Latin America in Transition:
Problems in Training and Research

LATIN AMERICA IN TRANSITION

Problems in Training and Research

Edited by

STANLEY R. ROSS

STATE UNIVERSITY OF NEW YORK PRESS

Albany

Published by State University of New York Press
Thurlow Terrace, Albany, New York 12201

ISBN 0–87395–068–2 / LC 71–112607

MANUFACTURED IN THE UNITED STATES OF AMERICA BY
THE RIVERSIDE PRESS, INC., CAMBRIDGE, MASSACHUSETTS
DESIGNED BY JOSEPH W. KRUGH

Contents

Acknowledgments

This volume contains the proceedings of a conference, held at the State University of New York at Stony Brook, 22–23 March 1968, devoted to the problems in training and research in a changing Latin America. The editor would like to take this opportunity to note that the Stony Brook Conference was made possible by the support and encouragement of the State University of New York Center for International Studies and World Affairs, the Center for International Programs and Comparative Studies of the State Education Department of New York, and the State University of New York at Stony Brook. Acknowledgment is due also for their very considerable assistance to Dr. James McKenna, Assistant Dean of the College of Arts and Sciences at Stony Brook and to Mrs. Katherine Napper of the public relations staff of that institution who so ably handled the myriad details involved in arranging the gathering. The editor is indebted to his staff at the Institute of Latin American Studies at the University of Texas at Austin for the typing and retyping of the manuscript. Last, but by no means least, a word of thanks is owed to Mrs. Suzanne Burakoff and Mrs. Jocelyn Harvey of the editorial staff of the State University of New York Press for such improvement of the manuscript as they were able to achieve by convincing a stubborn editor.

Introduction

STANLEY R. ROSS In 1967 the State University of New York initiated a series of annual "Conversations in the Disciplines" as a means for the advancement and dissemination of knowledge. These conferences are intended to facilitate dialogue among the scholars of common interests scattered on the many campuses within the state system as well as to provide an opportunity for the exchange of ideas with leading scholars from other parts of the world.

Without taking a stand on the question whether or not area studies constitutes a discipline, the formulators of the program made the various area study programs within the State University of New York eligible for inclusion in the "Conversations" conferences. The interested faculty at the State University of New York at Stony Brook, aware that the rapidly changing *ambiente* in Latin America made urgently necessary a review and reconsideration of existing approaches to training and research related to the area, proposed that a "Conversation in the Disciplines" be held to discuss the problems involved.

The proposal was approved and the conference was held on 22–23 March 1968 at the Stony Brook campus. The gathering was made possible by the joint support of the State University's Center for International Studies and World Affairs, headed at that time at Planting Fields in Oyster Bay by Dean Glenn Olds, and the Center for International Programs and Comparative Studies of the State Education Department, ably directed by Dr. Ward Morehouse. A distinguished group of scholars, both North American and Latin American, accepted invitations to prepare papers, and more than one hundred faculty from units of the State University of New York and neighboring institutions attended the sessions and participated in the discussion.

The meeting was organized in three academic sessions and a dinner meeting. The former focused attention on three subthemes of the conference subject: training for research in Latin America, research opportunities and problems, and collaboration in research, both interdisciplinary and international. It will be noted that the format followed in the three sessions varied. Since there exist disciplinary variations in training problems, the initial session included principal papers representing the fields of anthropology, history, economics, and literature with a single commentary. The topics of the other sessions, research opportunities and problems and interdisciplinary and international collaboration in research, cut across disciplinary lines. Accordingly the format was reversed to consist of a single paper for each topic with a representational group of commentators from disciplines other than that of the principal speaker. Latin American scholars as well participated in the latter sessions enriching the discussion by bringing out the reactions of native scholars to foreign researchers. Dr. Leopoldo Zea, distinguished Mexican philosopher and Director of the Faculty of Philosophy and Letters of the National University of Mexico delivered the keynote address at the dinner meeting on the subject "Identity in Latin America."

At first glance it may seem that Dr. Zea's paper is quite general and does not treat directly the same problems as the other essayists. However, it does relate to the other papers and, at times, quite precisely. One of the noteworthy characteristics of a changing Latin America has been the growing consciousness of identity or at least a conscious search for something that is called identity. It is demonstrable that this development very significantly affects the subject discussed at the Stony Brook conference—namely, the matter of training and research as they relate to people working and studying in relationship to this hemisphere.

Nationalism is very clearly one of the dominant characteristics of developing Latin America. Professor John J. Johnson has observed that "the most important single phenomenon in Latin America today is the rapid growth of nationalism."[1] Its manifestations are not only political and economic, but also cultural and intellectual. Indeed, much of the friction and conflict identified and the sources of resentment detailed by several of our speakers are related to a forceful and far-reaching intellectual nationalism. And the search for a sense of identity is an important, even an essential, ingredient of that nationalism.

The Mexicans have devoted the most attention to this problem in Latin America. In their famous search *"en busca del mexicano y lo mexicano"* persons from every type of intellectual activity and from every form of creative endeavor have taken part. Dr. Zea has been in the forefront of that effort, even going so far as to suggest the appropriateness of a national philosophy. In his paper, he discusses the historical development and present state of Latin America's search for identity. He shows that the United States has played a major, and primarily a negative, role in this development. It is his contention that the United States has hindered the development of an autonomous Latin America. Events from the Monroe Doctrine to Santo Domingo are the historical underpinnings of Latin American fear of the United States.

The key point is that any discussion of United States academic endeavors in Latin America must take into consideration the general role of the United States in Latin American history. Successful intellectual activity must be based on respect not paternalism, intellectual autonomy and not cultural imperialism.

The Camelot episode clearly demonstrated that a major problem confronting academic research in Latin America is posed by fears, both old and new, of the United States. It is very striking that time and again speakers—whether treating of training of researchers, research problems and prospects, or research collaboration—would refer to what must almost be described as the Camelot syndrome. The episode looms as a omnipresent specter whenever one talks about intellectual activity in Latin America and in association with Latin Americans. Since Camelot has cast a shadow which looms larger and more menacing than its original projection and since its implications enter into any discussion of research sensitivity or collaborative endeavors with Latin

American scholars, it would seem appropriate to summarize briefly the history of the Camelot Project and to identify some of the fundamental issues which it has raised. While the fundamental ethical problems—both political and academic—are discussed, concern here is principally focused on the effect of Camelot as it related to the difficulty or ease with which North American investigators have access to research materials in Latin America.

The academic community in general and Latin Americanists in particular are indebted to Professor Irving Louis Horowitz for the most systematic and penetrating examination of the rise and fall of Project Camelot.[2] His volume provided the main ingredients of the brief discussion which follows. This study not only contains the basic documentation on the Project, which is quite revealing concerning the subtle changes which the official position underwent, but also Professor Horowitz's own information-packed and thoughtful appraisal of the fiasco. Finally, the volume contains essays by participants, observers and outraged commentators who run the gamut of the political spectrum and of possible reactions to Camelot.

In 1964 in response to a Department of Defense request for an evaluation of its research and development programs, the Defense Science Board criticized various deficiencies in the behavioral research program. Partly in response to those criticisms and partially as a reflection of its responsibility for administration of the military assistance program and for research, planning and organization of counterinsurgency and limited wars, the Department of the Army through its contractor at American University, the Special Operations Research Office, set the wheels in motion for Project Camelot.[3]

On 4 December 1964 the project was described in a document sent to a select group of scholars, both in the United States and abroad:

> Project Camelot is a study whose objective is to determine the feasibility of developing a general social systems model which would make it possible to predict and influence politically significant aspects of social change in the developing nations of the world. Somewhat more specifically, its objectives are *first,* to devise procedures for assessing the potential for internal war within national societies; *second,* to identify with increased degrees of confidence those actions which a government might take to relieve conditions which are assessed as giving rise to a potential for internal war; and *finally,* to assess the feasibility of prescribing the characteristics of a system for obtaining and using the essential information needed for doing the above two things. The

project is conceived as a three-to-four year effort to be funded at
around one and one-half million dollars annually. It is supported by
the Army and the Department of Defense . . .[4]

And so began the largest single grant for a multidisciplinary social sciences research undertaking—one which terminated less than a year
later amid a torrent of criticism, some of it justified but much of it
based on emotion and misinformation.

Even the very term Camelot has a variety of explanations. Some have
attributed the label to President Kennedy's partiality for the musical
comedy, while an unkind critic has suggested that "for the Army it was
happily symbolic of the knight in shining armor come to slay the
dragon of disorder—and so gain half the kingdom."[5] Professor Kalman
Silvert, noting that in coloquial Spanish, *camelo* means joke or jest, reports that after its demise Camelot was often referred to in Latin
America as Project Camelo(t). He adds that *camelo* also is perilously
close to *camello*, or camel, "a notoriously nasty beast."[6]

The scholars who became involved in the effort were anxious to contribute to the development of a social science with contemporary relevance. Camelot was viewed as a legitimate opportunity to do unre-
stricted basic research with unprecedented funding of a relatively
unlimited nature. Some were uncomfortable under military sponsorship,
but this discomfort was rationalized by the hope that their efforts
would serve to educate the military and, hopefully, orient it to a constructive role. While some of the leading planners had hopes that their
efforts might contribute to the avoidance of major revolutionary up-
heaval, none of them viewed their role as one involving espionage.[7]

Professor Robert Boguslaw, a senior social scientist recruited for
Camelot by its director, Professor Rex Hopper, joined the effort too
late to influence it before its demise. He was aware that the Army was
notorious for maintaining close scrutiny and direction of the design,
content and course of research conducted under its auspices. However,
he writes that he

> finally became convinced, . . . that Camelot was accepted as a *bona
> fide* departure from this policy—that it was indeed to provide an op-
> portunity for social scientists to conduct an unprecedented and enor-
> mously significant study in the field of social change.[8]

It remained for a member of the staff of the Special Operations Research Office, Theodore R. Vallance, to endeavor to clarify the nature

of Project Camelot, which he called "the largest, most ambitious and probably the most widely heard of—I will not say most widely known" and in the process reveal some of the reasons for the confusion and ambivalence which colored it. He emphasized that Camelot was planned as "an objective, non-normative study concerned with *what is* or *might be* and *not* what *ought to be*."[9] He declared from the start the project was planned as basic research, with no obligation to deliver a product which would have application to anything but further research and development activity. The Research Office justified its undertaking to its superiors as a *feasibility study only.*

However, Vallance concedes that one of the basic difficulties was the two divergent supporting arguments within the Defense establishment. On the one hand there was prideful defense of the basic scientific nature of the research undertaking. On the other hand was the necessity of convincing skeptics of the utility of the effort in confronting pressing current practical problems represented by insurgency, national liberation movements and social turmoil. Small wonder that even very good outside observers should be victims of confusion as to the true objectives of Camelot.

It was in Chile, in May 1965, that a rapid sequence of inflammatory newspaper accounts of spying, outcries of academic outrage against being recruited for espionage under the guise of legitimate research and congressional investigation brought Camelot to a noisy end. It is ironical that in the preliminary Camelot documents, Chile was not included in the list of "model" nations to be studied. However, Camelot's directors asked Dr. Hugo Nuttini, Assistant Professor of Anthropology at the University of Pittsburgh and former Chilean national, to explore the suitability of Chile as a case study and to sound out Chilean scholars on their willingness to collaborate in the effort. Nuttini never was a regular member of the Camelot staff. Nuttini never identified the United States governmental agencies sponsoring the proposed project, a fact well known to the scholars who had received the preliminary project design and which was made available to Chileans from other sources. When the story broke in highly sensational form, Nuttini, who contrary to instructions had given the impression that he was an official of Camelot authorized to make proposals and arrangements, persisted in contending that he had been ignorant of the Department of the Army's role and that he had been duped.

The May 1965 United States intervention in the Dominican Repub-

lic appeared as timely proof to critics who viewed the United States as
an interventionist and counterrevolutionary force in the hemisphere.
Espionage and intervention were regarded as appropriate terms to be
applied to Camelot by a wide range of Chilean political opinion. Communist Jorge Montes speaking in the Chilean Chamber of Deputies
declared that

> the project reveal(s) the determination on the part of the United
> States foreign policy to intervene in any country of the world where
> popular movements might threaten its interests. To this end, they use
> a covert form of espionage, which they try to present in terms of scien-
> tific research, thus violating the most elementary norms of sovereignty.[10]

However, he was not alone. Miguel Ortiz, Chilean Foreign Minister,
warned against allowing the economic and social programs of the
Alliance for Progress to be overshadowed "by strategic considerations
of fighting non-existent insurgency."[11] A responsible and knowledgeable
journalist like John Chamberlain referred to Camelot as an intelligence
operation in the 14 August 1964 issue of the *Washington Post.*[12] And
Senator Fulbright observed that "as any sensitive observer might have
anticipated, the Chilean government . . . took offense at this project,
with its implicit connotations of counterrevolution and possible intervention."[13]

The United States Embassy in Santiago, knowing nothing of Project
Camelot, made clear to the Chilean government its lack of prior knowledge and its acute embarrassment. It gradually became clear that the
Department of State was unhappy with the entire undertaking and that
there was a jurisdictional dispute involved between the State and Defense Departments. For the Chileans, it appeared as evidence that the
"Pentagon" was determining United States Latin American policy. It
was increasingly clear that Camelot would have to go, and the Defense
Department announced that Project Camelot was being cancelled "on
the grounds that its original doubt about the practicality of officially-
sponsored research on other nations had been verified by the reaction
in Chile to the news of the project."[14]

It is worthy of note that Project Camelot was cancelled on grounds
that it was inadvisable rather than in terms of its feasibility. Much of
the public criticism has focused on the political aspects and implications and the inept and untimely handling of the project rather than on
its content and some of the very serious questions of academic ethics

involved. A group of Argentinian sociologists endeavored to focus attention on the scientific shortcomings of Camelot in a letter protesting the project addressed to the *Revista Latinoamericana de Sociología*. After describing the shock and incredulity produced by a reading of the project description, the Argentinians noted that

> We are not going to enter into considerations about the political aspects of the project. . . . The least that can be said is that the political decisions which define the utility of the data to be gathered explicitly presumes interference in the internal affairs of the Latin American nations. In the present note we are interested in emphasizing the academic implications of a project of this type in the context of Latin American sociology.
>
> In this sense we believe that it is our obligation to declare that the nature of the project damages directly the principles of professional ethics in so far as it affects the theoretical and empirical autonomy of the investigator.
>
> . . . In the mentioned project the ideological orientation is not incorporated as a source for the development of hypothesis, but is purely external: data is projected, gathered and analyzed for its direct utility to the goals of politico-military purposes quite independent of the theoretical and empirical concerns of contemporary sociology. . . . The problem area focused upon . . . undoubtedly can be explored from a variety of ideological orientations. What is inadmissable is the combination of these aspects in a program of investigations in our countries sponsored by the armed forces of a foreign power and the resulting data will be of immediate practical application in the formulation of foreign policy decisions for that country.
>
> The formulation of a project of this type very seriously affects the objectives of many sociologists desirous of institutionalizing in Latin America a serious, rigorous and professionally responsible scientific tradition which would include an ample and rich international collaboration, and raises serious doubts about the objectivity and scientific value of such cooperation. For a clear professional conscience the Camelot Project does not permit hesitations, the political purposes are enunciated explicitly and without ambiguities. . . .[15]

While some of the foregoing assertions appear of questionable validity, the letter does touch upon some key disabilities of Project Camelot and does raise some critical questions affecting the scientific and ethical implications of the undertaking. Unquestionably much of the confusion arose because of what Professor Horowitz had described as the "ambiguities" which beset the research proposals for Camelot. Two additional considerations are clear—namely, that most of the difficulties arose and an almost hysterical response was evoked because of the sponsorship by the Department of Defense and the association of the research with Cold War politics, and that insensitivity to the political *ambiente* prevented those involved from anticipating foreign reaction, which made disastrous consequences almost inevitable.

Project Camelot raised once again in dramatic form ethical questions which have been confronting social scientists for some time. What is the relation between science and policy? Does acceptance of assignment for the government, and more particularly for certain branches of the government, automatically impair the independence so essential for the flourishing of scholarship? What are the limits to probing the viscera of another society, particularly when the investigation is being sponsored by and conducted on behalf of another government?

Professor Herbert Blumer of the University of California, Berkeley, identified three serious threats to scientific integrity implicit in agency-directed research: "1) the restraints imposed on the scientific pursuit of truth; 2) a disrespect of the rights of the human beings being studied; and 3) an unquieting corruption of scholars engaging in agency-directed research."[16] Time and again the differentiation comes down to the contrast between grant and contract research. Professor Horowitz himself underscores the dangers of the sponsor's stipulating the ends of the research, which then poses a question whether the data gathering process is determined by social science needs or by governmental needs. He argues most persuasively for the importance of preserving the "autonomous character of the social sciences disciplines" in the "pursuit of the larger demands of society."[17]

The increasing politicization of the social sciences both in the United States and in Latin America makes questions of sponsorship, objectives and sensitivity all the more complicated. In Latin America itself much of the current social sciences research has a strong policy orientation and, of course, ideological presumptions are not without a role.

Project Camelot unquestionably has provided a handle for those wishing to criticize the United States and all its activities abroad. It has made access to research materials more difficult for the United States investigator and introduced an increased degree of caution on the part of Latin American researchers in regard to collaborative endeavors. Survey projects and those involving quantitative data collecting have been made much more difficult and, in some instances, impossible.

The United States government was concerned about the consequences of Camelot in another area—its effect on the conduct of the foreign relations of the nation. In the interest of preventing repetitions of Camelot, President Johnson, on 2 August 1965, noting that some Federal Government-supported social science research could "adversely affect United States foreign relations," asked the Secretary of State to take steps to "assure the propriety of Government-sponsored social science research in the area of foreign policy."[18] Two days later Secretary Rusk commented before a Congressional subcommittee:

> We are aware that large and invisible official United States projects probing into delicate social and political matters may, unless they are carefully planned to take full account of foreign sensibilities, help to create or increase hostility not only toward researchers identified with the United States Government but also toward American scholars who are completely unconnected with Government agencies. We must take care that official sponsorship of research does not increase the difficulties of independent American scholars who are doing or plan to do private research abroad.[19]

The Department of State concluded that the Camelot affair "dramatized the fact that Federally-sponsored studies infused with political meaning may well not be viewed by foreign intellectuals and political leaders as exercises in detached scholarship." And the Department report quoted sociologist Robert A. Nisbet to the effect that "when a major Federal Department—be it Defense, State, or Commerce—sponsors a scientific project . . . it is elementary that not even the elixir of scientific method is sufficient to wipe out the fact of sponsorship."[20]

The result of these concerns was the establishment in September 1965 of the Foreign Research Council in the Department of State. It is the province of this body to review all foreign research projects funded with government funds. There were those who expressed concern that the new review procedures represent a new threat to free inquiry. However, it should be noted that the so-called "basic" research agencies and programs—National Science Foundation, National Institutes of Health, National Institute of Mental Health, the Fulbright-Hays programs and the National Defense Education Act—are exempted from the Council review procedures. In many of these areas the State Department is involved by statute. In addition, classified studies conducted without field work or contact with foreign nationals are normally exempted from formal review. Other types of projects involving field work abroad or a significant amount of communication with foreign nationals must be cleared in advance by the Council.[21] During its initial three years of operation, this institution has functioned primarily to evaluate and reorient politically sensitive projects. It thereby has paid attention to an element deserving serious consideration in the evaluation of individual projects whether sponsored by the government, or by universities, research centers, or foundations.

In this area, as with other problems raised by the papers presented at the Stony Brook conference, definitive and all inclusive solutions are not to be expected. However, it does seem that certain valid guidelines might be suggested. Our Latin American colleagues legitimately can expect and even demand of us clean credentials and academic competence. And those responsible for the preparation of and dispatch of researchers to the other parts of the hemisphere can do no less than insist on these two conditions. We must also insist that graduate students and more advanced researchers work only in the area of their professional competence and that each be expected to maintain professional integrity and conduct himself and his research with a sensitivity to the host environment.

It is vital that every single researcher—be he graduate student or senior scholar—have as thorough a knowledge of the area as possible and that he really be equipped to do what he is proposing to do. The idea that social science researchers with professional competence in their respective discipline can be retooled easily and quickly to apply their knowledge in Latin America should by now be recognized as a naive assumption which leads, almost inevitably, to the most grotesque mistakes.

Qualified scholars usually have a fairly sound appreciation of what would constitute a sensitive and therefore unfeasible research undertaking in their field in a given area of Latin America at any given time. However, it would be useful to consult with Latin American scholars and research institutes about the appropriateness of any particular project when doubt exists. It also would be helpful to advise researchers to seek an affiliation with a Latin American institution. The nature of relationship would vary with the circumstances, but in any event it would give the United States investigator a base for his studies, provide the mechanism for access to qualified Latin Americans and their views and would result in an open and fruitful intellectual tie to the mutual benefit of the visitor and his hosts. Since Latin Americans have been turning to Europeans as a means of diversifying their academic contacts and on the assumption that such collaboration might be less likely to be complicated and tainted, it would seem appropriate wherever possible in collaborative research ventures to seek a triangular arrangement involving Europeans, North Americans and Latin Americans.

Turning to the three academic sessions, it is noteworthy how clearly the discussion of research training, of research problems and opportunities, and of interdisciplinary and international collaboration overlapped. Time and again the speakers referred to the effect that both politicization and polarization of Latin American intellectual circles and the continuation of research projects associated with certain United States governmental agencies would have on the research climate. Similarly this problem is further complicated by the inundation of Latin America by swarms of investigators, by the intellectual imperialism and scholarly mercantilism which has tended to characterize their efforts and by fundamental divergences among Latin American and North American scholars in the evaluation of "significant" and "relevant" subject matter for investigation.

In all three sessions ably chaired by Professor Pedro Carrasco of the State University of New York at Stony Brook, Professor Marvin Bernstein at the State University College, Fredonia, New York, and Professor Frank Carrino of the State University of New York at Albany, the participants whether speakers or commentators tried to grapple with these dilemmas faced by United States investigators. The most spirited audience participation occurred at the second session when several exiled Cuban scholars endeavored to "politicize" the session by criticism of the Zea dinner address and of the Castro regime. The liveliest discussion among session participants was evoked by the stimulating and provocative essay by Professor Silvert in the final session of the meeting.

The participants discussing the training of researchers for a changing hemisphere found it difficult to escape from the conditioning influence of the research climate and environment and the recognized deficiencies of present programs and move on to systematically constructive solutions. However, some concrete suggestions relevant both to training and research conduct do appear. Virtually all of the participants observe that the recent affluence of North American institutions has enormously increased the amount of support for training and research on Latin America. However, all agree that while the results have been impressive quantitatively, they have been less striking in terms of quality. Professor Morse suggests that we should have learned that it is not enough to have more scholars, more books, more funding, more visitors, more teaching aids, etc., to insure the ripening of Latin American studies. Professor Adams points out that increased numbers have not broadened the types of research conducted by trainees and research scholars. Speaking of the policy sciences, Professor Blair summarizes the situation by describing the returns meager, competent personnel in short supply, teaching antiquated, productivity low, innovation almost absent, data grossly inadequate and systematic analyses scandalously rare.

Several of our speakers commented on the increasing specialization which has come to characterize the various disciplines. As the social sciences have become more and more specialized and differentiated, the training of new researchers has become more narrow and the communication between disciplines more difficult. Professor Dauster, speaking for the field of literature, observed the very complicated problem of providing the student with mastery of a broad subject matter including both Hispanic and Latin American literatures at the same time that he acquires a near-native fluency in the languages. His comments also reflect the generation-old conflict between *peninsulares* and *criollos* which, in this discipline, has been an added hurdle to the growth of qualified persons and their effective training.

There may be noted a general disillusionment with the concept of area studies and the training of students in this form. This has been reflected in the general pattern of North American institutions, which generally have tended to move away from area degrees toward disciplinary programs. The editor shares Professor Morse's disenchantment with contrived and forced interdisciplinary efforts. He has had comparable experiences with "polite and tortuous strategies" for integrating the disciplines, which only lead to reinforced segregation. These views are echoed by Charles Wagley and Magnus Mörner, both of whom believe that the day of the area specialist is over. The latter called for trainees and scholars to excel in their respective disciplines and set standards of training and criticism sufficiently firm to insure quality. For, as he noted, if the scholar does not possess a firm grasp of his own discipline, his smattering of knowledge about other aspects of the area is of little scholarly value.

Professor Dauster, while appreciating the utility of area studies, feels that the present programs in his field do not do an adequate job of training potential scholars. He emphasizes the importance of a strong disciplinary base—"the scholar is a man trained in a discipline equipped to investigate the complex spectrum of problems which occur within that discipline." What, if any, place remains for area studies?

Speaking for himself, the editor believes that there is little question of the utility of a broad multidisciplinary program for undergraduates and for terminal master degree candidates. In these cases the area concentration affords more flexibility and a broader grasp of hemispheric problems that might be obtainable within a single discipline. The program must be designed with some rational base to avoid the supermarket random selection of courses. At the doctoral level, though, grounding within a discipline is essential not only for meaningful research training, but also for the pragmatic consideration of academic placement. If an area degree can provide the equivalent of a discipline doctorate plus exposure to a second discipline, the benefits should be greater.

Many research undertakings require some familiarity with the techniques and knowledge associated with other fields. Equally important is that the beginning scholar have some appreciation of the capabilities of fields other than his own. A useful device is the development of the interdepartmental "problem seminar" where discipline-prepared students and faculty examine a significant developmental problem from a range of disciplinary points of view and employing their respective techniques.

Supporting area courses and seminars offer the only hope of mitigating the enforced specialization that proper disciplinary preparation increasingly requires. The need for area base and background becomes even more pressing when we consider Professor Adams' identification of the supradisciplinary type—the mathematician, the systems theorist and cyberneticist—associated with the increasing technification and quantification of the social and policy sciences. To expand on Howard Cline's comment, something must be done to avoid complete divorce from the people and the land.

Professor Mörner, fully aware of the difficulties of keeping pace with the information explosion in any given field, let alone maintaining knowledgeability of other disciplines, endorses Wagley's idea of the desirability of "cultural brokers" who periodically would summarize research in one discipline for the benefit of others. A similar purpose, he observed, would be served by periodic interdisciplinary conferences.

While Professor Wagley warns that the recent affluence may not endure long, thereby solving the problems posed by sheer numbers of investigators inundating the lands to the south, at present the wave of researchers headed for Latin America remains a very real problem. The magnitude of the invasion—which Professor Wagley described as virtual saturation—tends to produce a sense of burden and impatience illustrated by the report that the Mexicans have been considering the establishment of a Research Service Center where all foreign investigators would be required to register.[22]

The key to mitigating this problem is to be found in Professor Alatorre's commentary. He suggests that Latin American reaction is very much conditioned by the nature of the proposed research, the method of conducting the research and the preparation and intelligence of the researcher. It is his contention that if these aspects are favorable, the researcher will be welcome. Time and again, the conferees reiterated the importance of the competence of the investigator. He must be well-trained in his field of specialization and be undertaking a project which lies within his area of competence.

Apart from the prerequisites of adequate preparation and competence, worthy of special note is Professor Morse's plea to restore the cultural focus which he fears is being lost in the heavy emphasis that our society places on the cognitive faculties. While this ingredient is most obviously needed in History and related humanistic fields, Professor Morse is convinced that even the social sciences would benefit from a focus on culture and values. Professor Morse, clearly an exponent of what he preaches, eloquently calls for articulateness or the recovery of the incipient scholar's ability to write in his own language with economy, precision and suppleness.

Several of our participants, including Professor Morse, warn the young researcher going to Latin America for the first time to avoid intellectual arrogance. They note the existence of highly qualified researchers in Latin America who have made and are making substantial contributions in their respective fields and to organized and productive research centers. The *caveat* to the student invaders is to avoid assuming the position of being the blind trying to lead the one- and two-eyed.

Turning to the actual conduct of research in Latin America, the conference participants were ever conscious of the conditioning climate. In one form or another, different speakers noted the atmosphere of suspicion, fear and anxiety. Professor Wagley referred to Latin American nervousness about the probing of sensitive areas. Professor Adams observed that research in Latin America is complicated by the bifurcated historical political role the United States has played and by the extreme polarization of political views in Latin America. He added that the beginning researcher and his mentor both have to be sensitive to the highly politicized situation.

The technification of the social sciences has resulted in at least two problems identified by our speakers. Professor Adams warns against cultural mercantilism resulting from the concentration of social sciences hardware in the United States, serving as justification for the shipping of research data to this country for processing without provision for sharing data and results of analysis. His colleague, Professor Blair, warns that while the new technology increases our ability to gather and manipulate data, it must be applied correctly to prevent deception or the introduction of new jargon for what is old hat.

The academic environment into which the North American researcher is going evidences some changes which must be noted. Professor Silvert calls attention to the fact that Latin American social sciences have been growing both quantitatively and qualitatively. Institutions of higher education have begun to provide research support for the empirical social sciences, and some private or semi-private research institutes of real significance have been developed. Despite these encouraging developments there remains a very real need for the multiplication of qualified social scientists in Latin America, where few if any are able to devote full time to research activities. There is need for increased training opportunities, including fellowship support for graduate study abroad and support for research that is conceived, carried out and reported upon by Latin Americans. It should be possible to build into North American research undertakings training opportunities for young Latin Americans as well as full participation by Latin American colleagues.

Only limited attention was paid by participants to the improvement of research facilities, but somewhat more was said about the need for improved data with which to work. The Rockefeller Foundation provided a start on the ordering and preservation of key archival centers, and recent microfilming efforts should help to preserve some parts of the vast materials which are deteriorating in different parts of the hemisphere. Professional organizations in the United States have recently shown concern for the gathering of quantitative data. Following the lead of the American Historical Association, the Conference on Latin American History established a Subcommittee on Historical Statistics. In 1969 the Joint Committee on Latin American Studies of the Social Science Research Council and the American Council of Learned Societies decided to support the preparation on basic bibliographical studies on economic history and, hopefully, substantive research studies as well.

It is in the area of topics of research that the chasm between North Americans and Latin Americans appears to widen. There is more than a suggestion that North American students are tending to follow in their mentors' footsteps and that the resulting research is remote from what the Latin Americans are experiencing and considering important. Professor Adams notes that new areas of research are being opened up by socio-economic development which are of interest to Latin Americans and which are only slowly being recognized by North Americans. Latin Americans complain that most North American research topics lack utility at best and at their worst are subversive. North Americans sometimes complain both of the abstruseness and the excessively applied character of Latin American research. Perhaps another differentiation is that made by Professor Zschock, who spoke of the holistic approach of Latin Americans as compared with the particularistic approach of North Americans.

Professor William McGreevey of the University of California in a recent appraisal of research on economic history wrote that North Americans have sought to present a more unified, satisfying and quantitative analysis and description of the economic past of an area while Latin American economists have been searching their past for the roots and causes of present economic development and problems.[23] Clearly there is a question here of the definition of what is relevant. Professor Wagley, in another study of social science problems and research in Latin America, noted that as a result of the presence of so many urgent social and economic problems in Latin America the social sciences are in great demand as useful instruments of social change.[24] In the same volume Merle Kling, the political scientist, called upon his colleagues to modernize, while economist Carlos Massad underscored the trend toward policy-oriented research, which he considered the preference of most economists in Latin America.[25] Sociologist Rex Hopper added that practitioners in his discipline were going into empirical and theoretical fields never before cultivated.[26] It would appear that the research topic gap may be narrowing. A concluding observation on the topical issue is Professor Fals Borda's comment that Latin Americans increasingly are tackling delicate subjects and producing studies critical of their societies, which may contribute to the defining of their identity in the sense Dr. Zea advocates.

A few other conference comments on research topics deserve to be singled out here. Professor Blair declared that the field is surfeited by general descriptive works, isolated in terms of time and place, and based on excessively routine data, largely uncoordinated and unevaluative and of limited use. He defines the need for good economic theory and tools of analysis for tackling the problems of growth. Professor Wagley, intensely aware of the climate of research, felt that the time is not propitious for large-scale team efforts, but that it would be better to concentrate on highly specialized, individual research which would produce new monographs, based on new data and offering new theses. Professor Alatorre differed with Wagley, and by his examples perhaps was suggesting that individual versus team efforts might depend on the field and the particular setting of the research at any given time.

The final topic of the Stony Brook conference focused on the question of collaborative research. Despite Professor Kalman Silvert's prefatory disavowals of his intention to be provocative, explaining that he is "getting to be a more tired than angry middle-aged man and also because somehow internally I never have the intestinal turmoil which seems to equal the verbal turmoil,"[27] he was indeed provocative. Cognizant of the topical chasm and the relevancy previously discussed in this introduction, Professor Silvert suggested that perhaps collaborative research might best be reduced or avoided *if* the price of such research meant Latin American determination of the topics to be researched. Quite correctly, Professor Silvert regards this as a serious invasion of academic freedom and like its converse—United States dictation of Latin American research undertakings—too high a price to pay for collaboration.

Professor Silvert drew strong responses from his commentators. Professor Fals Borda feels that collaboration is both possible and desirable if the partners move within the same frame of reference and abide by the same social commitment. He emphasized the need for an honest partnership. Professor Stanley Stein felt that the healthiest collaboration tended to come when the Latin Americans sought on their own terms to solve their own problems. This still would permit mutually satisfactory collaboration over broad areas. Professor Stein warned that collaboration must not be predicated on concepts of intellectual empire. One cannot help but feel that the kind of direct dialogue which occurred between Professor Silvert and his United States and Latin American commentators should lead to more fruitful collaboration.

The editor can only add that collaboration is working in the Joint Committee on Latin American Studies program of collaborative grants, which originate from joint proposals by United States and Latin American collaborators with the essential condition imposed that the two investigators be of comparable qualifications and that equality of role be maintained. A few other suggestions by conference participants in this connection are worthy of repetition. We already have noted the importance of multiplying the number of qualified researchers in Latin America through the incorporation of a training component for Latin Americans in North American research projects and by providing expanded graduate training fellowship opportunities. In connection with the latter, it is important to avoid contributing to the "brain drain" problem in Latin America. Unfortunately, "brain drain" is attributable not only to the seductive attractiveness of higher salaries and more favorable working conditions and facilities, but also to recurring conditions in Latin American countries interfering with the freedom essential to academic pursuits.

In this day of AID and foundation development contracts, Professor Blair recommends that institutional ties be established which will be responsive to Latin American hopes and ambitions and not merely represent the creation of practice grounds for North American academics. During the discussion at the Conference, Dr. Cline suggested that large-scale projects be organized on a counterpart basis, namely incorporating an equal number of Latin Americans and North Americans. Efforts to draw into such undertakings European researchers will be responsive to Latin American desires to diversify their research contacts and will lessen concern about subservience to North American scholarship and political goals. More meaningful collaboration will result when efforts are made to provide effective training so more Latin Americans may make use of data and if that data and the results of analysis of it are made readily available to interested Latin Americans.

As is so often the case, the Stony Brook Conference tended to focus attention more on problems than on solutions. When suggestions were made they were usually in the form of concrete and constructive criticism and advice to the United States researchers, organizers of research and educators. However, it is to be hoped that the frank discussion of the issues involved and the various constructive proposals will promote in the Latin American studies field a searching reappraisal of the problems of training, research and collaboration in the light of a rapidly developing and changing hemisphere.

Institute of Latin American Studies
University of Texas, Austin
May 1969

NOTES

1. John J. Johnson, "The New Latin American Nationalism," *Yale Review* (Winter, 1965): 187.

2. Irving Louis Horowitz, ed., *The Rise and Fall of Project Camelot: Studies in the Relationship Between Social Science and Practical Politics* (Cambridge, Mass.: Massachusetts Institute of Technology Press, 1967), pp. 3–44. Professor Horowitz earlier published a briefer version of his study in *Trans-Action*, 3, no. 1 (1965).

3. Dante B. Fascell, "Behavioral Sciences and the National Security," in Horowitz, ed., *op. cit.*, pp. 184–85.

4. "The Design and Purpose of Project Camelot-Document Number 1," in Horowitz, ed., *op. cit.*, pp. 47–48.

5. Marshall Sahlins, "The Established Order: Do Not Fold, Spindle or Mutilate," in Horowitz, ed., *op. cit.*, p. 78.

6. Kalman H. Silvert, "American Academic Ethics and Social Research Abroad: The Lesson of Project Camelot," in Horowitz, ed., *op. cit.*, p. 82n.

7. Horowitz, *op. cit.*, pp. 6–8.

8. Robert Boguslaw, "Ethics and the Social Scientist," in Horowitz, ed., *op. cit.*, p. 110.

9. Theodore R. Vallance, "Project Camelot: An Interim Postlude," in Horowitz, ed., *op. cit.*, pp. 203–05.

10. Jorge Montes, "A Communist Commentary on Camelot," in Horowitz, ed., *op. cit.*, p. 232.

11. Horowitz, *op. cit.*, p. 14.

12. Cited by Jesse Bernard, "Conflict as Research and Research as Conflict," in Horowitz, ed., *op. cit.*, p. 128.

13. J. W. Fulbright, "America in an Age of Revolution," in Horowitz, ed., *op. cit.*, pp. 199–200.

14. Horowitz, *op. cit.*, p. 16.

15. *Revista Latinoamericana de Sociología,* Vol. I, No. 2 (July 1965): 251–55.

16. Herbert Blumer, "Threats from Agency-Determined Research: The Case of Camelot," in Horowitz, ed., *op. cit.,* p. 117.

17. Horowitz, *op. cit.,* p. 32.

18. U.S., United States Department of State, Foreign Affairs Research Council, *A Report on the First Three Years* (August 1968), p. 1.

19. *Ibid.*

20. *Ibid.,* p. 4. The Nisbet quotation is from an article entitled "Project Camelot: An Autopsy," which appeared in *The Public Interest,* No. 5 (Fall, 1966): 59.

21. *Ibid.,* p. 8.

22. United States Office of Education, "United States University Activity Abroad: Implications of the Mexican Case," *Reports Digest,* No. 37 (November 1968), p. 5.

23. William P. McGreevey, "Recent Research on the Economic History of Latin America," *Latin American Research Review,* III, no. 2 (Spring 1968): 89.

24. Charles Wagley, ed., *Social Science Research on Latin America* (New York: Columbia University Press, 1964), p. 28.

25. Merle Kling, "The State of Research in Latin America: Political Science," in Wagley, ed., *op. cit.,* p. 207; Carlos Massad, "Economic Research in Latin America," in Wagley, ed., *op. cit.,* p. 238.

26. Rex Hopper, "Research in Latin America in Sociology," in Wagley, ed., *op. cit.,* p. 282.

27. Transcription of Professor Silvert's introductory remarks, recorded at the Stony Brook Conference.

Identity in Latin America*

LEOPOLDO ZEA

Latin America. What is it? Who is it? What countries make up that part of the continent known by that name? Today, this aggregate of countries is considered a part of the underdeveloped or developing world. Latin America is also included in the so-called "Third World." Does it resemble the countries of Asia and Africa, and if there are possible similarities, are there also special and specific differences? Latin America embraces, of course, what is called "Hispanic" America, that is, the countries which resulted from Spanish colonization. In addition, it includes Brazil, that huge portion of South America colonized by Portugal, which together with Hispanic America gives rise to the term "Ibero" America. Moreover, this part of America receives yet another name," Indo" America, limited, naturally, to the America of strong indigenous or mestizo population. The term "Latin" America claims to be more comprehensive and is based on the Latin origin of the colonizing countries, including the French.

* Translated by Professor J. B. McKenna and Mr. E. J. Bebko.

Today a new designation is urgently needed, one which can no longer be racial or cultural, but economic. I refer to the appearance in America of new nations no longer simply Latin, Spanish, Portuguese, mestizo, or indigenous in origin, but of African or Asian heritage and Saxon—more precisely French or Dutch—cultural background. That is, peoples of the new nations which are emerging in the Antilles. Their cultural formation is different from that of the "Latin" American countries, but not their economic, political, or social configuration. They share a common colonial origin as former colonies of the Old World of Spain, Portugal, France, England, and Holland. In a broader sense, they were colonies of the so-called Western World. In this respect this part of America, taken as a whole, reveals a specific relationship with what is called the "Third World," for it forms a part of that group of nations considered underdeveloped or developing.

From the above point of view, the United States of North America shares the same origin: a colony of the Old World, a consequence of westward expansion. It differs in that it has moved from colony to colonizer, has created a new imperialism, and has established itself as the leader of the forces of the Western world, continuing to expand and dominate as it fills the "power vacuum" left by the withdrawal of the old leaders of the West, the imperialist powers of Europe. This origin and subsequent development, the transition from colonial to imperialist nation, has given rise to a two-fold sentiment in relations between the United States and the countries of Latin America: admiration and rejection. Admiration for the country that has freed itself from colonial status and become a model of the possibilities for development. On the other hand, rejection of the nation that has forgotten these antecedents and created a new empire, simultaneously closing off the opportunity for other countries to follow its exemplary path. Within the United States a similar two-fold sentiment characterizes its relations with the Latin American countries. The United States knows it is an example, a great moral example, but at the same time it sees itself destined to create a great empire, to lead and direct the world of which it was once an instrument. It fuses these attitudes as it considers itself not only an example to be followed, but also the indispensable guide along its chosen paths. It easily makes its own development the goal of all possible development, its objectives the objectives of all. The indisputable representative of the new world created by the West, it is at the same time its sole beneficiary.

The countries of Latin America develop an awareness of their identity and goals as a function of the identity and development of the United States. The ideal to be achieved by the countries of the south shortly after their emancipation from colonial status was expressed in the words of Argentina's Domingo F. Sarmiento: "Let us become the United States of South America." The central concern of Latin American educators and political leaders was to create an order similar to that of the United States, with its laws and institutions, and the formation of men who would make such an order possible and sustain it. They sought to create a liberal order and also to form the men who would make it possible, not merely creating free institutions but educating for freedom as well.

In the course of this quest, Latin Americans came to realize the distinctions between their origins and the goals they seek, goals embodied by Saxon America. Political emancipation of the colony will not suffice; it must be accompanied by mental emancipation. The habits and customs inherited from the colony must be relinquished for the habits and customs that have made progress possible in the western world and which the United States so extraordinarily embodies. Only this change would enable Latin America to enter the path of progress in a manner that would not be one of mere subordination. This, more or less, was the thrust of Latin American thought at the beginning of the second half of the nineteenth century, a thrust which underlines the intimate relationship that, in one way or another, the two Americas, Saxon and Latin American, will maintain.

Along with the initial attitude of proselytizing admiration comes a growing realization that the powerful archetype follows in the course of its natural development paths not precisely those of Latin America. Moreover, these paths lead the powerful nation toward expansion, first and foremost, at the expense of its neighbors. Bolívar had already called attention to the differences between the interests motivating the two Americas and the lethal consequences that would result from alliances between countries of unequal powers. "One wishes to imitate the United States," said the Liberator, "without considering the differences of elements, of men, of things." Elsewhere he wrote, "Having once formed a pact with the strong nation, the obligation of the weak nation becomes eternal. Taking everything into consideration, we will have tutors in our youth, masters in our maturity." If Latin America was to achieve the same goals as the United States model, it would have to do so by its own efforts. No other nation would do for Latin America what it could not do for itself. Diego Portales, Chilean dictator, warned his America about a doctrine like the Monroe that made the United States not only the archetype to be followed, but the very arbiter of the destiny of the Latin American countries.

Toward the end of the nineteenth century, although their admiration for the United States did not diminish, Latin Americans began to consider the need for developing for themselves the North American's institutional and educational structures in order to strengthen themselves and avoid falling victim to the voracity and growth of the "Colossus of the North." In order to put an end to anarchy, revolutions, and internal wars, it would be necessary to adopt rapidly the habits and customs of the men who had built the United States. "We must urgently become the Yankees of South America," said Mexico's Justo Sierra, "and we must do so quickly, because the giant that is growing closer and closer to us as a result of the industrial and agricultural might of its frontier states tends to absorb and dissolve us should it find us weak." This is the same defensive spirit that appears in José Enrique Rodó's parable of Ariel and Calibán. It will be necessary to imitate and follow the powerful nation to the north, but only in that which will serve the development of the Latin American countries, assimilating Calibán's material strength but keeping him always at the service of Ariel. Ariel is presented as a symbol of the Latin American spirit, as the expression of an aggregate of countries that, using one instrument, pursues its own goals. Ariel's goals are not Calibán's, although Calibán's strength may serve Ariel's purposes.

In the early years of the twentieth century the old fears are borne out. The United States no longer bears the slightest resemblance to the nation that in the eighteenth century had thrown off the yoke of colonialism to offer the free world a body of doctrines and institutions affirming the rights of men and nations. Now it is a nation that claims the right of hegemony over a world the great imperialist powers of Europe had divided among themselves. The United States of William McKinley and Theodore Roosevelt demands a new division of the world and, as part of this, hegemony over Latin America as a "private preserve" for its interests. It demands a new interpretation of the Monroe Doctrine which will prohibit the presence of other imperial forces that would oppose the natural expansion of United States forces. And there in the South, facing this destiny which the powerful nation has assigned itself, stands a group of nations forced no longer merely to imitate but now to resist their model. They realize that mere imitation of laws and institutions will not suffice to make them free and powerful. Nor will the imposition of a determined type of education, such as the one inspired by positivism, be enough for the formation of men similar to those who span the United States from frontier to frontier. Adopting certain legislation and institutions has not been enough to bring forth a social class capable of doing for Latin America what the great western bourgeoisie has done for the United States and the powerful nations of western Europe.

Liberal dreams in Latin America evaporate in the face of reality impossible to conceal. The hopes of making Latin America the United States of the South end up as but one more utopia. The social, political, and economic realities of this America have not changed. The countries of Latin America are still marginal nations, mere instruments of another's progress and development. It had been hoped that a bourgeoisie could be created in Latin America modeled after the class which had brought about progress in the western nations; instead, it became a social group which in order to subsist had to serve as instrument, intermediary, figurehead, or clerk for the interests of the great western bourgeoisie. Far from using their wealth for their own development, the Latin American countries use it as a means for other nations' development. The social groups which are aware of this situation know also the obstacles in the way of change. In order to achieve the envisioned development, they will be forced to confront on the one hand internal colonial forces that could not be rooted out by imitation of the laws and institutions which had brought about the greatness of the United States and the western world. On the other hand, they will have to confront the forces that built those countries and will not permit any competition that might limit them. It will be necessary to face simultaneously the aggregate of internal interests that feel prejudiced by the rise of any new interests, and the powerful external interests that would likewise feel limited should forces capable of competing with them appear. In other words, they would have to confront national conservatism and international imperialism, united to obstruct the rise of any force that might interfere or compete with them.

The United States of the early twentieth century is able to obstruct the appearance of forces that might threaten its hegemony over Latin America. Those days mark the alliance between its interests and those of conservative groups who fear a change of order unsuitable to their best interests. Old Latin American evils are transformed into instruments for the maintenance of United States hegemony over the continent. Figureheads and dictators appear, charged with maintaining the order best suited to the expansion and development of the new imperialism. Opposing them there will appear in Latin America the nationalist movements that on the international level will be called anti-imperialism. This nationalism will appear in various forms in Latin America, as a defensive nationalism quite distinct from the one that inspired the imperialist expansion. The Mexican Revolution, begun in 1910, will be the first great expression of this nationalism, concerned with developing internal strength capable of resisting external attacks. Similar movements, some continental in character, will follow, such as the APRA in Peru, *Varguismo* in Brazil, Peronist *justicialismo* in Argentina, the Bolivian *Movimiento Nacionalista Revolucionario*, Venezuela's *Acción Democrática*, and others, all nationalist movements of differing doctrinal inspiration, blends of socialism, liberalism, corporativism, and even fascism.

They will all share the common concern, as it was liberalism's concern also, for the creation of a bourgeoisie, that would do for Latin America something similar to what a similar class did in Western Europe and the United States. Yet it will be precisely the liberal failure in this regard, since liberalism resulted in a series of oligarchies alienated from national reality and development, which marks a new orientation that proposes to be more realistic and seeks its support in the unchanged reality of Latin America. The new Latin American social group which hopes to mold itself into a bourgeoisie knows it can no longer follow the path taken by the groups which created the great western bourgeoisie, whose fruits were capitalism and its inevitable imperialist manifestation. The middle classes or groups in Latin America which aspire to a role similar to the one played by the bourgeoisie in Europe and the United States will be unable to claim, as does the United States a readjustment in the division of the world. Quite the opposite, these Latin American groups know that, far from being an active participant in this readjustment, Latin America is simply an object of the readjustment begun in the early twentieth century, a battlefield of alien interests, a part of the world consigned to fall under a specific hegemony.

The Latin American social groups will have to react precisely against this reality. They know they obviously cannot aspire to a new division of the world since there is no longer anything to be distributed and, moreover, that they—their countries, their wealth, their realities—are the object of that distribution. The only thing they can hope for is to impede it. It is not a question of forming new empires, as in the case of the United States, but of forming nations, independent and autonomous, that will no longer be the objects of divisions among the imperialist powers. The middle groups in Latin America, where the forces for the formation of a series of national bourgeoisies are recruited, do not think in terms of empires, nor even of internal national hegemonies. They know that an attempt to do this led to the failure of oligarchies like the Mexican *Porfiriato,* which caused the great revolutionary explosion of 1910.

These social groups seek development, but they know that it can only be achieved by internal means. There are no more countries to be found in other latitudes to pay for the development of the Latin American bourgeoisie what the countries of Asia, Africa, and Latin America itself paid for the development of the western bourgeoisie. Nor can the masses of the Latin American countries themselves bear this burden; the disastrous experiences of the oligarchies proved that. It will be impossible to create any wealth or prosperity based on the misery of their own peoples. In Latin America such efforts on the part of the oligarchies led to revolutions and unrest.

Therefore, it would be necessary to equalize sacrifices and benefits, not permitting disproportionate amounts of either to fall to any one class. Mexico's Adolfo López Mateos, while campaigning for the presidency of the Republic, offered a concise summary of the policy to be followed in countries like Mexico: "The final development of our fatherland requires sacrifices that cannot be asked of only one group of Mexicans while others reap the benefits. Sacrifices and rewards, as part of our rapidly growing and constant development, must be shared equally."

Latin American nationalist movements strive for this equilibrium by advocating a series of social reforms designed to raise the social and economic level of the great masses that would necessarily have to serve as the base of the prosperity of the nation's bourgeoisie. There would be no market for this class's products among ignorant and impoverished masses, and where else than among its own citizens would national industry find markets? For decades foreign markets had been preempted by the products of international capitalism. More than sense-less, it would be suicidal to compete with the latter. The only possibility was their own nation, a nation that would be a poor client if its masses continued to lack the basic requirements for subsistence.

This explains why the groups who hoped to become a national bourgeoisie interested themselves in agrarian, labor, fiscal, educational, and health reforms. Not philanthropy, this was a pure and simple case of caring for and nurturing the "hen that lays the golden eggs." In any event, the reforms would in no way be so extensive as to threaten the basic goal of development and prosperity for the national bourgeoisies. The purpose of the reforms was merely to create the conditions required for development of a national market that could absorb the products of the industries to be created by the would-be bourgeoisie. Sacrifices? Yes, but a bit more equally distributed. Benefits? Of course, but insuring that some of them would reach the social groups responsible for their creation.

This policy would be opposed on two fronts: by the oligarchies determined to maintain a system of exploitation similar to the one established by the metropolis over the colony, and by the interests of the new imperialism, unwilling to be limited or constrained by the aspirations of Latin American national bourgeoisies. Strengthening the latter would imply losing markets and investments that heretofore had benefited only the international bourgeoisie. This would lead to a competition imperialism was little disposed to accept. Therefore, agrarian and social reforms, such as those undertaken by the Mexican Revolution in 1917, the revolutions in Guatemala in 1954 and Cuba in 1961, the MNR-led revolution in Bolivia, Vargas in Brazil, Perón in Argentina, and other similar movements in Latin America would immediately encounter two-fold opposition, from within, on the part of the oligarchy, and from without, especially from the United States. World War II, waged against Nazi Fascism and Militarism, gave great impetus to Nationalism, not only in Latin America, but also in Asia and Africa. At the same time it caused a strong reaction on the part of those international interests which felt endangered.

Anxious to avoid reforms that might affect them in the slightest way, these interests viewed them as a function of the Cold War being waged between the United States and Russia, between the capitalist and communist ideologies. Without realizing it, Latin American nationalists, like nationalists in other parts of the so-called Third World, found themselves militating in the communist camp. The internal oligarchies and the propaganda of foreign interests depicted their social and economic reforms as dangerous and open concessions to communism. Their leaders began to be accused of being extremists; "filibusterismo" and military "golpismo" were encouraged as means of closing off even those minimum reforms granted to sustain "the hen that lays the golden eggs."

The first nation to suffer this type of coup was Guatemala, then Cuba, except that the latter in order to survive openly threw itself into the arms of Communism. Pressure in Brazil led to Vargas' suicide, Jânio Quadros' resignation and Goulart's expulsion. Peronism was persecuted in Argentina because of its implications for social reform. Encouraged by United States interests that feel threatened by such reforms, "golpistas" appear wherever these reforms are even proposed. Nevertheless, the presence of John F. Kennedy in the White House and Cuba's resistance, which culminated in an open declaration of faith in Communism, will lead in North America to a policy that tends not only to recognize the practicality, but also the urgent need for reforms that will raise the social, economic, and cultural level of the peoples of Latin America: the same minimum degree of reforms Latin American nationalists had been struggling for.

This is the purpose of the Alliance for Progress. After all, even capitalism is nourished by the "eggs" of a "hen" that must not be allowed to perish. It is not an altruistic act, but one deemed necessary for the maintenance of the capitalists' own progress and prosperity. The Alliance for Progress offers material aid for Latin American development, contingent upon implementation of a series of social, economic, fiscal, health, and educational reforms, those minimal reforms nationalist groups in Latin America had long been struggling for. Nationalists and reform-minded United States capitalism coincide. In this way, each seeks its own goals: creation and strengthening of national bourgeoisies, and assurances that the prosperity of the great international bourgeoisie, United States capitalism specifically, will be maintained. Benefiting the great Latin American masses will serve both interests. In the final analysis, it would be a means of tying the destinies of the Latin American bourgeoisies to United States capitalism in return for a minimum of concessions.

But would this solution suffice? It assigned only a passive role to the masses. Certain improvements were doubtless sought, but only if they did not threaten the interests of the forces that permitted and made such improvement possible. It was oriented toward attaining certain goals which could in no way be forgotten. Nonetheless, a series of internal and external circumstances were making the masses of Latin America, as well as Asia and Africa, aware of their situations. The least favored and most exploited of Latin America's social groups had accepted the leadership of the middle groups insofar as it furthered their own development. But they also realized the limits inherent in committing their aspirations exclusively to their leadership. That is, they realized that the social reforms which they needed would never be implemented in direct response to their needs, but only as a by-product of the interests of the national bourgeoisies. The great Latin American masses were beginning to realize that what they could not do for themselves would never be done for them by other social groups or interests. The Cuban Revolution was an example of what could be accomplished in spite of the enormous difficulties and sacrifices it demanded. The Cuban people had claimed a little more than had been allotted and thus encountered the hostility and resistance which other Latin American countries had previously encountered when advancing similar claims. This attitude would produce as a counterpart the fear that the kind of concessions proposed by nationalist groups and the Alliance for Progress, far from stopping any socialist trends, would instead stimulate them. This concern would cause any social reform, whatever its goals, to be viewed with hostility. A repetition of the Cuban experience was not to be permitted in Latin America, and it could not be avoided if social reforms which led to further and more dangerous demands were encouraged.

One result of such an attitude was to be the "cuartelazo," such as the military's revolt against President Juan Bosch of Santo Domingo in 1963 because he had dared to implement the reforms stipulated by the Alliance for Progress as prerequisites for its aid. João Goulart of Brazil fell in 1964 having tried to realize similar timid reforms. The phenomenon of "gorilismo" will find encouragement wherever the threat of social reform—no matter how limited—appears. In the context of the Cold War, not only nationalist reforms, but the Alliance for Progress itself will be seen as a beachhead for communism. Senator Robert F. Kennedy referred to this situation in a speech delivered to the United States Senate in 1965, in which he condemned the United

States invasion of Santo Domingo in support of the "golpistas" who two years earlier had overthrown President Bosch: "our determination to stop the communist revolution in this hemisphere must not be interpreted as opposition to popular movements which rise up against injustice and oppression merely because those who are the target of these popular revolutions accuse them of being inspired or directed by Communists. In any event, we know that revolutionary forces have the support of many non-communist democrats."

In spite of such a spirit of understanding of the social needs of Latin America, which many North Americans share, United States government policy still seems to be directed toward ignoring these needs or dealing with them in a spirit of tutelage. Consequently, an increasingly clear awareness is developing in important sectors of opinion of the Latin American countries that their future is separate and distinct not only from the native social classes that have claimed leadership roles, but also from the forces of United States capitalism. In turn, the social groups in Latin American referred to herein as national bourgeoisies relinquish their national identity for open and full commitment of their destiny to that of United States capitalism.

At their stage of development, the Latin American bourgeoisies find that the opportunities offered by the national market, always small and composed of miserable and impoverished Latin Americans, are no longer sufficient. To move from light to heavy industry requires association with United States capitalism. They will be poor and subordinate compared to the powerful United States partner, but richer and more powerful than the other groups of their own nation. The drive is no longer for national industrialization but for formation of industries subordinated to the interests of a larger society, capitalism, which in order to continue its development needs to create more powerful industries in areas of the world, like Latin America, where heretofore simple exploitation of raw materials had sufficed. Concern for national development is abandoned in favor of private or group development in the context of international capitalism. It is no longer a question of trying to resemble the United States or any other powerful western nation, but rather of becoming a part of them and their destiny in return for a broader and more complete private development. This is the tendency in recent years in various parts of Latin America, especially in those areas where "golpismo" has eliminated the most determined followers of the groups who dreamed of creating national bourgeoisies that would do for Latin America what their counterparts had done for Europe and the United States.

The Latin American bourgeoisies that nationalists dreamed of at the beginning of the twentieth century seem to become a thing of the past, as the nationalists commit themselves to international capitalism, led now by the United States. The social groups to whom the nationalist bourgeoisies looked for support of their development become more aware each day of their divorce from that class, and of a relationship that transcends national limits. Seeking to fortify themselves, the nationalist bourgeoisies, not only in Latin America but in the rest of the underdeveloped or developing world, had formed a somewhat romantic and idealistic bond of solidarity which the 1955 Bandung Conference tried to make a reality under the designation the "Third World." Just as in Latin America, the leaders of this world have been disappearing, forced out by the same pressures that had eliminated Latin American leaders. There, as in Latin America, the social groups that had at one time aspired to create nationalist bourgeoisies were either eliminated or else became mere interest groups that sold out to international capitalism. Nonetheless, that ideal form of solidarity called Third World made the great masses, in whose name the leaders spoke or claimed to speak, aware of their transcendence and universality: there are many other peoples in the world who have been and are being exploited as instruments of the grandeur and prosperity of alien interests.

These social groups, which until yesterday were considered mere instruments, become aware of the chasm separating their interests and those of the social groups that gave them minimum concessions in order to further their own development. Aware also that these social groups at their present stage of association with international capitalism will do nothing for other social groups, however large these may be, that will not serve their own concrete and specific interests. Thus, as a response to the association of Latin American bourgeoisies with the development and destiny of international capitalism, there arises a kind of solidarity which could be called popular, that is, between peoples, between various sectors of those great masses whose development seemed to depend on the development of the class that wanted to become a bourgeoisie.

And the nation which now encourages this new form of solidarity in

Latin America is Cuba. Cuba, the nation forced by internal and external pressures to declare its solidarity with the countries of the world that had chosen the socialist solution, tying its destiny to that world. A new form of solidarity encouraged more by example than by her instruments of propaganda. On the other hand, the cold war propaganda, which the United States has used to justify blocking social reforms which might prejudice the interests of various of its most privileged groups, has awakened in those who have been so lightly accused of being communist agitators interest in doctrines to which they had previously been indifferent. And in order to satisfy this curiosity, the accused find a justification for their social concerns that now transcends the national limits in which they had first been posed. A new form of socialism which is not precisely the one supported by the U.S.S.R. or China begins to appear in Latin America as a natural response to the divorce created between the interests of the great masses and those of the middle classes who aspire to become bourgeoisies. With the latter obliged to tie their destiny to international capitalism, the great masses tend to unite on an international level with other masses in a similar situation.

Has Latin America reached the point where its various social groups must make a definite choice between capitalism or socialism? I do not think the choice must be so complete, that is, between forming part of the United States or the Russian or Chinese orbit. But a new type of society will have to be formed, valid perhaps not only for Latin America, but for other countries in similar situations. A type of society which corresponds to social reality and which cannot merely imitate once more alien social forms. Socialism? Of course, but perhaps a socialism that will safeguard the individual values Latin Americans have always guarded so jealously. A new form of community, not merely association, would not be foreign to Latin America. Since the days of Bolívar her best spokesmen have referred to it as an ideal to be strived for, although they have never really defined it.

The Changing Scene of Behavioral Science Research in Latin America Today: A North American View

RICHARD N. ADAMS

Introduction. Of the many ways in which behavioral science re-search is changing in this hemisphere, I want to select one for particular attention and touch briefly upon another. The latter, of no less importance than the former, but hardly unique to the hemisphere, is the fact that the very nature of the behavioral sciences is changing. Of particular importance in the present context, however, is that they are becoming politicized. Before turning to these two matters, let me review the question of the degree to which the behavioral sciences are political. Let us distinguish three phases of science: subject matter; practice; and methodology. In the selection of subject matter, science is thoroughly political. By this I mean that the political context of the scientist *always* sets limits as to what he may choose to study, and it is often the case that such consideration gives specific direction to the choice of topics. Certain subjects will be proscribed, and from the remaining available field, specific topics will be preferred. Until recently in the United States, politics dictated that social scientists could not study Castro's Cuba; the State Department would allow newsmen to visit that nation, but refused this privilege to social scientists. Today, many governmental agencies concern themselves with whether experimentation may be carried on with certain kinds of drugs. The government has decided that materials necessary for detailed investigations into the death of President Kennedy will not be available to social scientists and historians. And so on. The list may be compounded for other countries as well as for the United States.

The practice of science is also clearly political in character. Whether science is to be carried out by individuals, small teams, or large, who may participate in these teams, where laboratories are likely to be established, whether a given scientist can be looked on as sane, are all matters that clearly involve politics. Since most large scientific installations depend upon government funding, the political decisions as to whether loot should go to Berkeley, MIT, or the University of Texas are matters that wander around in the minds of senators and congressmen, as well as scientists and university administrators. The issue is whether political advantage may be had by the choice of one set of practices as against another.

With respect to scientific methodology, the role of politics is less clear, but it cannot be said to be entirely absent. It can be argued that the thing known as "scientific methodology," in its abstract form, may be said to be apolitical. In a broader meaning, however, methodology includes a decision to accomplish a specific goal and to use criteria to judge success. Just as topics of research have political limits, so goals and criteria of specific research may be influenced by political factors. Since, in sheer quantity of manpower and time, most scientific research in the United States is of this goal-oriented kind, it follows that it may be subject to political influences.

The Changing Nature of Social and Behavioral Sciences.   Since 1945, the social and behavioral sciences have grown in their own technology, the scale of their operations, and the complexity of their disciplinary interrelations. The availability of recording devices and the general technicalizing of interviewing and observing have made the mere process of getting data a matter of some sophistication. For handling the increased body of data that is thereby available, the computer has become an almost indispensable adjunct to the work of many social scientists.

A concomitant of technological growth in data gathering and analysis has been the scope of the research operation. In the United States, national samples indicate what may be the trend of activity among 200 million people. Survey research has long since convinced politicians and public alike that social science has evolved into a meddling network of doorbell-ringing students and housewives. Behind this expansion in interviewing lies extensive organization, capital, and, above all, a sufficient pay-off that not only keeps the whole process going, but that constantly generates new enterprises. I do not think that it is anti-intellectual to suggest that the very emergence of this kind of thing, coupled with integration into national life, reflects an economy of abundance in which the choice has been to spend more time on finding out what people like to eat rather than being sure that they have enough to eat. The appearance of this disjointed and sprawling investigative apparatus is a product of western industrialism, both in quantity and in its very design. And, as one anonymous social scientist suggested, ". . . we nearly always study the weak in our society—the cultural minority groups and criminal groups, for example, and what our findings reveal about such groups tends to reinforce the power of the strong."[1] This is a topic that deserves much more attention, but I mention it here merely to set the context of the present discussion.

Academic disciplines in the United States have also been undergoing important changes. On the one hand, they are becoming more highly specialized and differentiated, so that communication between them is increasingly difficult. The political scientist's formula to predict the direction of votes in the United States Congress is of relatively little professional interest to the linguist engaged in identifying new rules for language. Even the social anthropologist and sociologist, who should be the closest of intellectual kinsmen, often find themselves mutually incomprehensible. The effort to achieve greater interdisciplinary work has proved to be intermittent and of uneven value and to pose as many problems as it solves. There have, however, emerged a series of social scientists whom we might refer to as supra-disciplinary. The mathematician, the general systems theorist, and the cyberneticist are not concerned with subject matter as it has been defined in the classical disciplines, but with any series of human behaviors that can be subjected to analyses of the variety being devised in the abstract. This poses in the United States academic system a remarkable discontinuity. There continues to be in the universities a series of academic disciplines that determine the allocation of individuals in the social organization that fixes their salaries and rewards for professional work; and this particular structure of allocation and reward often has little to do with the fact that the real intellectual community to which an individual belongs is determined by his relation to the supra-discipline. This discontinuity is important because the individual working within a supra-discipline is especially dependent upon communication with his new scholarly community. He cannot work alone, as a single scholar, but must have repeated contacts with his fellows who live outside his own academic setting.

To summarize these points, then, we have in the United States a social and behavioral scientific system that is technologically complex and costly, highly focused on problems determined by the leaders within an industrialized capitalist society and increasingly structured professionally so as to require constant communication with colleagues who are geographically dispersed and dependent on centers of high technical and personnel capacity.

The Politicization of Social and Behavioral Research.   The professionally trained investigator who wishes to work in Latin America will find that research has become increasingly politicized. Research, as was suggested above, is by its nature political. What is new is its increasing politicization throughout the hemisphere. It is primarily since the Second World War, and mainly in the last decade, that the political aspect of research has been brought to the level of consciousness. A person is politicized when he knowingly participates in a political process; and a science takes on this character when its practitioners knowingly recognize that their work has this kind of condition and significance.

While we can hardly exhaust the reasons behind this, I want to look at three interrelated phases of the process which, I believe, throw light on how it is happening in this hemisphere. There are: (1) changes in the academic situation in both Latin America and the

United States or, let's say, North America; (2) changes in the bases of research support; and (3) changes in the political context of research.

(1) THE CHANGING ACADEMIC SITUATION. The contrast between the Latin American social science research situation in 1945 and that of today can be summarized as follows. In 1945, there were almost no academic research organizations in Latin America, few university departments giving research-oriented training, no continental community of scholars in this area, and what minimal funding of any research there was stemmed from the government. In the United States, the war had stimulated anthropologists and rural sociologists to increase their research in some countries. Individual scholars carried out individual research projects, but there was limited interest in promoting wider research or in stimulating the development of research centers in Latin America.

Without going into the interesting and rather complicated history of the intervening years, we can contrast the above with the picture today. Latin America now has research centers of international repute and a core of economists, sociologists, anthropologists, and psychologists who are in the process of being supplemented by young men of high calibre with advanced training from foreign centers. Universities are competing in establishing centers to the degree that there are already more in name than there are qualified scholars to staff them. The community of specialists has so evolved that not only do Argentinians work in Chile, Peruvians in Venezuela, Guatemalans in Mexico, but there has recently been formed a council of Latin American research organizations composed of over thirty such institutions to promote, coordinate, and facilitate the increasing growth of social science in the area. There has developed an aristocracy of Latin American social scientists who cite each other's publications, see each other frequently at international meetings, and comprise the core of this growth.

In the United States, a sudden spurt in Latin American studies interest began in the 1950s, primarily under the impetus of Ford Foundation support, and this continues in modified form today. The National Defense Education Act supplied many universities with funds to upgrade and expand their curricula in Latin American language and area studies. The expansion in United States graduate programs by the early 1960s was reflected in increasing numbers of professors and students who flooded into Latin America to carry on research or quasi-research. Team research became more common, and with it an increasing use of the growing technology of the behavioral sciences. The hardware of this new technology of the behavioral sciences, however, generally remained in the United States because it could neither be readily funded nor manned abroad. This expansion had many aspects of a kind of cultural mercantilism, where the raw materials of information were gathered in Latin America, often with the participation or assistance of Latin American scholars, but the results were sent north for processing. As with classical mercantilism, the products, in the form of books or monographs, could then be bought in both North and Latin America, but their cost was such that they were in short supply in the latter area.

While this expansion was stimulated in part by an increase in available federal funds, the government also expressed its interest in other ways. The anti-communist mania was increasingly manifest in government circles, and the Defense Department and C.I.A. increased their activities along with those of the State Department. Funding for research began to appear in unlikely places, and some members of the United States academic community found it impossible to resist the lucrative support offered by some of these agencies. The pay-off came, of course, with the Camelot affair, and with it an outburst of Latin American reaction to this changing situation.

Legitimate Latin American scholars had increasingly been smarting under United States academic mercantilism. The Camelot affair brought this irritant into conjunction with real and imagined political concerns about United States academic imperialism; what had been scattered complaints and concerns began to evolve into a widespread suspicion and, in some instances, outright rejection of United States academic activities.

Latin American centers of quality today are often dependent upon foreign funding, either from international agencies or other countries, most importantly, the United States. It is not clear whether this dependence upon externally derived funds will change sharply in the next few years or not. The foreign dependence probably modulates what might, in other circumstances, develop into more clear-cut nationalistic rejection of foreign researchers.

These changes in the hemisphere mean that the foreign scholar wishing to carry on research in Latin America must take the necessary pains to work within the on-going scholarly community of the country in which he is researching. The painful examination to which United States social science has been subjecting itself over the past few years has necessarily included problems of work in foreign areas. The United States is still financially a dominant power; its social scientific establishment is the largest and best paid in the world. But the kind of product this community has turned out is certainly not universally admired, and some portions of it are regarded with some contempt. The United States scholar must be more sophisticated as to where his own efforts stand in the wider world of academic and scholarly work; he must recognize that access to greater establishment facilities is not equivalent to access to greater truth. The community of scholars, while ideally independent, in fact is deeply affected by national variables. This was not so apparent in Latin America twenty-five years ago; it is clearly evident today. The difference between the academic research expansion in Latin America and that of the United States emphasizes these differences.

(2) CHANGES IN RESEARCH SUPPORT. Whereas research support in Latin America has always been primarily dependent upon the government, United States government support of research in the social and behavioral sciences has expanded both in quantity and in variety since the Second World War. The National Science Foundation and the National Institute of Health have been particularly important in this. The Office of Naval Research, always interested in a variety of basic research topics, has continued to some degree with its support, especially in an area such as geography. The State Department, most in need of effective understanding of other countries, has been most backward and disinterested in the possibilities of research. Partly because of the ignorance that permeated State Department activities, the Department of Defense felt that it was necessary for it to extend its own inquiries into the nature of Latin American societies.

The expansion of research from the private sector took a sharp upswing when the Ford Foundation finally decided to move into the Latin American field toward the end of the 1950's. The linkage of foundations with the government that entered the public eye with the appointment of Dean Rusk as Secretary of State and matured with McGeorge Bundy's presidency of the Ford Foundation raised the serious question as to what degree public and private fund sources were in informal cahoots, complementing one another.

From the point of view of preparing for research today, this expansion of funding and the interlocking of private with public sources poses some serious problems. In the first place, the growth of funds has promoted the cult of large-scale research. There are students being turned out today who cannot imagine how to carry out research apart from such a situation. While not intrinsically evil, this poses a number of problems when funds become scarce. Furthermore, the public-private linkage means that any large-scale research is likely to be assumed to have governmental approval, even if the funds can be demonstrated to come entirely from private sources. A large expenditure from a private source is not likely to be made in the United States if, in fact, it is contrary to the interests of the government, as currently expressed.

In my own recent research experience, where I was overtly using funds from both the Ford Foundation and the AID, my Latin American friends would comment to me that they knew that I was really from the C.I.A. but that it was all right because they had known me for a long time! I am not encouraged by the reception that I might expect elsewhere. The bases of research support today have, in fact, become so centralized that it makes little difference to many Latin Americans whether real support of a specific project comes from such a centralized source or not. An assumption of association may be readily made where there may be none in fact.

There is no easy resolution to this problem. It affects the research of Latin Americans too, although it is obviously more significant in the work of United States scholars. It is also my impression, however, that while uncertainty and suspicion may exist, in most instances this does not bring the matter to a head. I will treat these dilemmas later.

The most obvious consequences of the expansion of research support has been the increase in numbers of people carrying on investigations. This, unfortunately, has not led to a comparable broadening of topics, but rather a concentration of more people studying more or less the same topics. This has meant that new research areas, opened up by the fact of development within Latin America, have been very slowly recognized because professors have followed their own line of interest and sent students to follow in their same old paths. Topics of interest to the Latin American countries have often been ignored in favor of topics defined by the state of the art in the United States. This has, unfortunately, its effect on Latin American scholars too, as Varsavsky[2] and others have pointed out.

The flooding of limited locales and research topics with United States scholars has become so intense that it is currently being investigated under a cooperative agreement between Latin American Studies Association and the Council on Educational Cooperation with Latin America of Education and World Affairs. The purpose of this study is to explore the range and effect of recent United States research efforts in three countries, Chile, Paraguay, and Guatemala, to clarify the dimensions of the research problem, and to explore the kinds of areas that have not been adequately defined as research areas. The dust raised by the Camelot affair unfortunately has not blown away; it has changed to mud.

The establishment of the Latin American Social Science Research Council (CLACSO) should in itself have a very beneficial effect on the direction of research. While it has as yet no special access to new funding, Latin American scholars will be better informed of the on-going research situation and will be better able to arrive at more rational and integrated decisions concerning their own research. The more far-reaching Latin American research may be, the more carefully North American scholars will have to adapt. Failure to do this will result in working at cross purposes, competing over topics in areas where perhaps a few or only one researcher can work effectively at a given time, and necessarily wasting research resources.

In this connection, however, let me voice partial dissent from those scholars who hold that research in Latin America should be directed by the national needs of those countries.[3] Insofar as research is sponsored by agencies interested in the national needs of Latin America or some specific country (and certainly if not most, many are), then there is every reason to have a set of national science policies. Unfortunately, however, scientific activity that is dictated solely by non-scientific concerns will, over the long run, weaken science as a whole.

What is needed in this regard, I believe, is a much clearer expression by responsible nations as to what kinds of research are necessary; as this becomes available, then people can be trained for those areas, and scientists can better find those particular topics that suit best their own talents. The issue, I believe, should not be to establish restrictive scientific policies anywhere, but to clarify and get support for national research needs. Scientists, by and large, will go where research support directs them to go. There must always be room, however, for individual and random exploration in scientific work, because it has long been demonstrated that important new discoveries will occur in unexpected places.

(3) CHANGE IN THE POLITICAL CONTEXT. While this paper cannot explore the changing world political context, it can single out a few processes that directly influence the Latin American research scene. I want to review a change in the United States policy situation and two major phases of change in the Latin American scene.

The foreign activity of the United States in Latin America, until 1932, was one of undisguised self-interest. At least from the time of John Quincy Adams, when Mexican territory was regarded as a legitimate object of United States expansionism, to the reoccupation of Nicaragua in the 1920's for the further protection of United States commercial interests, Latin America was regarded as a weak part of the international world. An important shift took place with the Good Neighbor Policy. This change, however, was a supplement and not a reversal of the United States position. This became clear when the United States once again used a strong arm to overthrow the Arbenz government in Guatemala in 1954. This, of course, was followed by the Bay of Pigs and Santo Domingo.

This recent phase of history can be characterized as a bifurcation of the face of United States policy. On the one hand, Good Neighborliness continues in the revised form of technical and economic aid and in the Alliance for Progress. But these efforts do not disguise the power position that resulted in the events just mentioned and in the continuing support of counter-insurgency, in the build-up of Latin American military establishments, and in the categorical rejection of the possibility of a real political experimentation.

The effect on the research situation of this dual-faced policy has been to reinforce the suspicion that any United States student or scholar may more represent the negative than the positive. Also, since these are, in fact, two faces of the single policy, it places special suspicion on the more positive efforts, a concern that has some structural substance.[4]

This political role of the United States is part of the large scene that includes important changes in Latin America. There are two aspects I want to mention here.

First, there is a polarization of political regimes in Latin America. The torrent of military coups of the past few years has brought to power a series of regimes that are basically either conservative or amenable to a conservative military. At the other end of the political spectrum is Cuba, well entrenched in complete political opposition to all other regimes in the hemisphere. The gap between the next left-most regime and Cuba is still very great.

In addition to this, there is over all of Latin America the much discussed phenomenon of nationalism. The self-awareness of a nation-state and the consequences for academic and scientific activity of this characteristic have received attention elsewhere.[5]

The combination of extreme political views and nationalism provides a setting which can place demands on the scholar's position as a researcher that may compromise or even destroy it under some circumstances. The way these restrictions are manifest may be seen in the factors that appear to complicate the research situation. These include the topics of research, the locale of research, one's own political or personnel background, ineptitude displayed during the research, and the particular background of the country involved.

Quite obviously, research into topics relating to political action, *guerrilleros,* private entrepreneurial ventures, private income, land ownership, individual taxation, political opinions, ideological differences of international significance, and related themes are much more likely to elicit negative reactions than are inquiries concerning the Mexican *corrida,* preceramic lithic industries, the Paraguayan ethno-history, or subtleties of linguistic change. In like manner, research that takes the investigator into areas of *violencia* or political unrest, even where the topic of research is quite innocent, may bring suspicion. The political and personal background of the individual is likely to bring difficulties if he is well known or makes a special effort to bring attention to himself. Each country has, at any point in time, its own political preferences, and it may find the political history of some student or academic threatening. The most common restrictions are among the more conservative regimes against individuals of communist or socialist backgrounds. Cuba is, so far as I know, the only country where a noncommunist background is a liability.

In addition to these factors, particular disciplines sometimes present problems. For example, the fact that social anthropology students were among the *guerrilleros* captured by the Argentine army a few years ago has given this field a dim reputation among the governing circles of that country. Social scientists in general are usually regarded with mixed feelings by politicians, since they as often as not are concerned with the misdirection or malfunctioning of political regimes.

The investigator wishing to work in Latin America today must recognize the importance of being adaptive. The environment throughout the hemisphere is changing. Not only is the Latin American scene undergoing important shifts, but the North American scholar appears to be wearing different spots. It is crucial to recognize these changes because the building of a real community of scholars, operating to some degree independently of the demands of the national systems to which individuals usually belong, can only take place through careful attention to the scholarly task and an open awareness of the real problems that each individual scholar must face in the accomplishment of his work. There is no ivory tower today; the scholar must equip himself and comport himself in the real political world. The future of scholarship depends on this being done effectively.

NOTES   1. Quoted by Gresham M. Sykes, "Feeling Our Way: A Report On A Conference on Ethical Issues in the Social Sciences," *American Behavioral Scientist*, X, 10 (June 1967): 10.

2. Oscar Varsavsky, "Scientific Colonialism in the Hard Sciences," *American Behavioral Scientist*, X, 10 (June 1967): 22.

3. See Varsavsky, *op. cit.;* and John Galtung, "After Camelot," in Irving Louis Horowitz, ed., *The Rise and Fall of Project Camelot: Studies in the Relationship Between Social Science and Practical Politics* (Cambridge, Mass.: The M.I.T. Press, 1967), pp. 281–312.

4. See André Gundar Frank's *Capitalism and Underdevelopment in Latin America* (New York Monthly Review Press, 1967). See also my *The Second Sowing* (San Francisco: Chandler Publishing Company, 1967).

5. See the papers by Adams, Boulding, and Varsavsky in *American Behavioral Scientist*, X, 2 (October 1967).

The Care and Grooming of Latin American Historians or: Stop the Computers, I Want to Get Off

In the United States the idea is still prevalent which thirty years ago threatened to destroy historical science in Europe—namely, the claim that history's only mission is to furnish an auxiliary service to sociology. . . . The antimetaphysical attitude of the spirit necessarily involves an antihistorical one. And indeed, the spirit of North America is fundamentally antihistorical, even though it supports a flourishing and magnificently organized historical science.

—J. HUIZINGA, 1927

RICHARD M. MORSE

The more I pondered today's assignment, the harder I found it to disentangle a report on the care and grooming of Latin American historians from general reflections on academic culture in the United States. Experience has taught me to head for the high ground. Had I been asked to prescribe for our discipline when I began teaching twenty years ago, my agenda would have been properly utilitarian and focused: more Latin American history in curricula, more Latin American historians on faculties, systematic Latin American library accessions, more faculty and student grants, more Latin American visitors, more paperbacks and teaching aids, more recognition of Latin American history by other specialists. Now that these blessings have descended in varying degrees of prodigality one realizes that, in T. S. Eliot's couplet:

> That is not it at all,
> That is not what I meant, at all.

One wishes not to be judged ungrateful to the entrepreneurs, organizers and philanthropoids responsible for our post-Fidel benefactions. But one recognizes with a start what should have been clear all along, that the hydroponic soil of academic subvention multiplies without necessarily ripening the fruits of scholarship.

In recent years I have found myself producing impressionistic, slightly disingenuous *pièces d'occasion* which speculate why Latin American studies are so indifferently cultivated in our country, given the resources and effort sluiced into them.[1] I have suggested that our backdoor exposure to the south conditions us to a peon-*pistolero*-busboy image which scares off sensitive young scholars. More important is a set of historic-cultural differences which block understanding —not simply for being differences but for being threatening ones. Parsonian categories help describe them, but what enables us to grasp their significance and gauge their historical momentum is the contrast between Church-type and sect-type societies elaborated by Max Weber and Ernst Troeltsch.

For all their unoriginality, my views have evoked flurries of protest, privately and in public. I have been accused of romanticizing Latin America, even personalizing it as a paramour; of insisting too shrilly on the relevance of the Thomistic heritage to contemporary Latin America; of being a cultural determinist; of being a counterrevolutionary; of deprecating American scholarship; of barking at (without daring to bite) the hand that feeds me; of being, in short, a "dangerous" influence. Yet the rejoinders so frequently stress how much rather than how well the guild is doing that a nerve may have been struck, however wobby the hand on the drill.

The matter of cultural focus is central to studying history and to identifying blind spots and resistance of fledging historians. Cultural focus is of course not an historian's monopoly. It is an obvious concern for students of Latin American literature and philosophy; but activity in this sector is still so esoteric in our country that history may soon have to sprout humanistic pinions if Latin American studies are not to flap in mournful circles on the lone wing of social science.[2] Social scientists in turn, although no strangers to the cultural realm, obey house rules which incline them more toward manipulation than toward reflection, toward generalization (reverentially called "theory") than toward morphology, toward indicators than toward metaphors, toward quantifying experience than toward rendering it. Such preferences are not necessarily mischievous. But in this case they seem better understood as cultural blinders than as noble scientific aspirations. Their side-effect on students is to separate them from subject matter, developing cognitive and manipulative "cool" at the cost of moral and expressive sensibility.[3] The absurdity of green undergraduates applying game theory to United States-Cuban relations or communications theory to Brazilian national development goes quite unchallenged.

What I label "cultural focus"[4] many social scientists prefer to call "values," a term redolent of the commodities market and suggesting lavish possibilities for transaction and exchange. A recent essay by Seymour M. Lipset, "Values, Education, and Entrepreneurship,"[5] perceptively analyzes the role of values in contemporary Latin America. Some reflections on this exemplary and influential statement may help me specify what I take to be the strategic contribution that historians can make at this juncture.

Professor Lipset aligns himself with those sociologists who stress the effect of values in fostering economic development. He is alert to the perils of determination, however, and of neglecting the extent to which values may be produced or sustained by economic factors. He appreciates the complexities of change, and the variety of situations that yield—and may even be encouraged to yield—innovation. Yet on certain counts his analysis requires the infrastructure which only history provides.

Like many others, Lipset regards "values" not as arrayed in a focus or matrix but as forming a cluster which, under modernizing pressures, can be picked apart like a box of Crackerjack. His value cluster includes "feudal social values," low achievement motivation, kinship ties and personalism, local community orientation, acceptance of traditional and aristocratic norms, paternalism, expressive behavior, aversion to manual labor, rural-type social structure, short-range profit calculation and non-professional intellectualism. By sociological definition, such values are antithetical to urbanization, industrialism, democratization and modernization. They are therefore eroding away in

Latin America, and with a little push from social engineers the transformation will be complete.

Now values like the ones listed can be reduced to discrete fragments of behavior. Once the "behavioral" scientist has tagged and patterned them, he relinquishes his job to the "policy" scientist (or else changes his own hat). It is a pity that these two types of practitioner, social cartographers and pundits, have usurped our social sciences. For neither is much interested in the deeper wellsprings of behavior[6]— that is, the realm of belief. Perhaps Americans shy away from belief as something private and unmentionable in our multisectarian society. Perhaps we confuse belief with dogma, and it offends our empiricism. Or perhaps our manipulative meliorism is to blame; because belief changes only glacially we prefer to deal with its ephemeral accommodations to circumstance in the form of ideology, behavior, values and style. Whatever its pathology, our fixation on ripples rather than tides (or, put less metaphorically, nipples rather than thighs) leads us to applaud reduction of family size, introduction of civil-service exams or investment in industry as though they signified "modernizing" shifts in a whole belief system.

Oddly enough, the antiseptic behaviorist who fails to distinguish belief from values ends up being more judgmental than the cultural historian. And when he arbitrates that Japan may retain its "traditional value system" because it is compatible with industrialism while a quarter of a billion Latin Americans must discard most of theirs, he is on his way to being an insufferable meddler.

A matrix of belief finds expression in shifting patterns of value and behavior. Otherwise it would have no permanence. It is not just since World War II or 1830 or 1760 that Latin American societies have exhibited transitional or contradictory or asymmetrical features. Since the Middle Ages and until now the Iberian world has experienced the tensions of traditionalism and millennialism, hierarchism and populism, localism and universalism, familism and individualism, hedonism and asceticism. It is in these historical terms that the travail of contemporary Latin America is best construed. However slapdash he may be as a psychohistorian, Vianna Moog has a sure instinct when he points Brazilians toward Aleijadinho as a culturally consistent therapeutic symbol and not toward North American or Japanese paradigms.[7]

A notable feature of Western cultural history for the last several centuries is the gradual consignment of belief systems to a subliminal realm. Social thinkers and political leaders have become progressively less able or more reluctant to tell us what they're up to—a fact easily confirmed when one compares the public utterances of Francisco Suárez and Celso Furtado, of Hernán Cortés and Fidel Castro, of Cotton Mather and David Riesman, of Roger Williams and Nelson Rockefeller. This subliminalization of belief gives margin for frenzied activity in the social sciences.[8] Although the practitioners assure us that they are laying bare the taproots of motivation and conduct, the reverse is more nearly true. That is, social science conceptualization tends less to illuminate social reality than to commemorate our growing estrangement from it.

One way to get at archetypal beliefs is from the premise that they have to do with the way that people imagine it possible to enter a state of grace, singly or collectively. On this score Max Weber wrote some pages which provide a passkey to social structure and social change in Latin America through the centuries.[9] But there is no need to be prescriptive. In a recent essay Fernando Guillén Martínez makes precisely the point of Latin American historical continuity—stressing the irrelevance to it of Western liberalism and Marxism—but with no use of Weberian categories. One could scarcely find a more dramatic contrast between historical and sociological outlooks than in the following views of Latin American industrial development. According to Guillén Martínez:

> None of these urban conglomerates [Mexico, São Paulo, Buenos Aires] could have reached its present physical size without the generalized use of the financial and manufacturing techniques of capitalist industrialism. But none of them shows a visible tendency toward political democratization or a lessening of social injustice. On the contrary, the old problems of authoritarianism, social inertia and violent struggle for power are more evident there than they were and still are in the old rural zone.[10]

Here is Lipset on the same topic:

> The value system of much of Latin America, like Quebec, has, in fact, been changing in the direction of a more achievement-oriented, universalistic, and equalitarian value system, and its industrial development both reflects and determines such changes. . . . Paternalistic feudal attitudes toward workers are characteristically more common in the less developed Latin American countries than in the more industrialized ones. . . . [The] more developed an area, the more "modern" the attitudes of its entrepreneurs. . . . Values clearly change as societies become economically more developed.[11]

My point is not quite the stark one that the Latin American is right about his own society and the North American observer wrong. More precisely, it is that the former's conclusions are plausible, while the latter's—however shrewd the observations which lead to them—are either platitudinous or wildly out of historical context. It is sobering to think that the American social science establishment is being mobilized for more of the same, but in leatherette rather than cowhide. Americans have always been patronizing toward the belletristic tradition of the Latin American *pensadores*. It is ironic that now, the very moment when social sciences have won their place in Latin America, American research is becoming so aim-inhibited that satirists and indignant polemicists (the Jules Faiffers, Russell Bakers, Norman Mailers, Paul Goodmans) promise to be our only intellectual sentries at the threshold of social reality.

By now it is clear that I do not propose to inventory the treasures which historical study holds in store for Latin Americanists. Instead I have seized upon what is for me its strategic role for the present moment and circumstances. At the risk of a perilous analogy, I can summarize by saying that the therapy which historians might provide for Latin American studies is similar to that which Freud brought to psychology two generations ago. Our social scientists and social engineers look upon Latin America much as Freud's colleagues regarded their parents—that is, as being in a state of hysteria, curable by hypnosis. Freud's genius was to perceive that "hysterical" symptoms had logical explanations in life-histories. "His method was to treat the long-past experiences and emotions as if they were still present in the adult; and the concept of the unconscious was the only thing that made this possible."[12] The Freudian exaggeration to which historians may fall prey is to overstress the importance of the early, formative years. But this emphasis is soon corrected in our activist age.

In the unlikely event that anyone accepted my diagnosis, I could expect to be asked: "Well, if that's the job to be done, how do we train up our students to do it?" The notion that every challenge or mystery in our physical, social or intellectual environment constitutes a "job to be done" or a "problem to be solved" is characteristically American. Its respectable name is instrumentalism. This outlook requires that the historical and moral personality of the observer be insulated from the challenge confronting him. It makes of scholarly activity what it has made of our military operations, a series of defoliations.

If for the moment we judge Latin American historiography by the criteria I espouse, it is clear that the Latin Americans themselves have been making memorable contributions. One thinks of such scholars as Mario Góngora, Néstor Meza Villalobos, Sérgio Buarque de Holanda, Indalecio Liévano Aguirre, Leopoldo Zea and Luis Villoro. The missionary spirit with which our graduate students invade Latin America sometimes produces the engaging spectacle of the blind attempting to lead the one- and the two-eyed. I do not, however, urge that Clio's apprentices abandon puzzle-solving and hard-nosed research merely to become gymnasts at dogging the footsteps, mounting the shoulders or falling at the feet of revered Latin American masters. The therapy must recognize cultural impediments to historical vision. It must restore sight to the "innocent eye" and to the "American eye."

The Innocent Eye. It is no commonplace to remark that American education cauterizes the candor and instinctual responses of its pupils. It beclouds what Sir Herbert Read calls "the innocent eye."[13] For verification I need only compare a school paper of my ten-year-old son with a term paper of most any graduate student. The historian Martin Duberman has, like his own students, been puzzled why eager, curious freshmen are turned into "protoypes of articulate emptiness"; why college years "do not initiate or further, but dampen or destroy efforts at self-exploration"; and why graduating seniors have not even begun to know "who the hell they are."[14]

Kenneth Keniston patiently explains this alienation, although ascribing more causative importance than a historian might to the demands of contemporary technological society. Our culture, he observes, places a premium on cognitive faculties ("capacities for achieving accurate, objective, practically useful, and consensually verifiable knowledge") and subordinates feeling, impulse, fantasy and idealism. In psychological terms this means that our schools must develop tyrannical ego strength in their pupils (or victims) at the expense of more affective or instinctual realms of the psyche.[15] The rate of psychological drop-out from this production line approximates the school desertion rate that we so much deplore in Latin America. The survivors who go on to study other societies are well equipped (or "trained," to use the title word of this symposium) to manipulate indicators and handle data, but they are grievously unfit to be historians.

To put the matter bluntly, our graduate schools discourage rather than cultivate qualities of mind required to write history and sympathize with other cultures.[16] I'm a bit perplexed, then, in addressing my theme—how to prepare historians for a changing hemisphere. For to request that our whole education system be dismantled and rebuilt to produce better Latin American historians is like asking Boeing to redesign the 707's and tool up again because the ashtrays are badly placed.

Elsewhere I have proposed that would-be Latin Americanists be exposed to scholastic thought, that they learn about casuistry and natural law so they can move in the historic intellectual universe of Latin America. I have proposed more intercontinental air-bussing of students to interrupt the academic ratrace. These are lackluster suggestions, however, because they ponderously insist on Latin America as a "field" of study. If students have yet to recover the innocent eye of childhood and earn the wisdom of maturity, they must be reintroduced— imaginatively, not merely cognitively—to the sexes, the passions, the poignancies of life, the ironies of action, the doggedness of will, the persistence of morality, the recalcitrance of society, the illuminations of faith. They must learn to see again—which means, for example, to read, to become lost in, Turgenev and Stendhal and Cervantes and Dostoyevsky and Melville. Notice I omit Latin American literature. This comes later, in solitude. Not simply because there are no Stendhals, but because of the cant about *costumbrismo* and *modernismo,* Machado's irony, Sor Juana's tensions, Unamuno's dictum on Sarmiento, and Carlos Fuentes' social criticism.

And somewhere in the land I hope that one stern but passionate preceptor might acquaint future historians with that open sesame to the Latin American world, Dante's *Inferno.* The *Inferno* is among other things a blazing geography of sin. And if there is one hallmark of Latin American societies which disconcerts and exasperates the American observer it is that the seven deadly sins still flourish there. Protestant America has tamed and renamed the sins. What is still covetousness in Latin America we domesticate as the profit motive; anger is a passing fashion of our youth (I believe the "angry generation" had a lifespan of two years); lust is for us an enfeebled "drive" coaxed into "healthy" bloom by psychotherapy; envy we call rising expectation; sloth is merely an extended coffee break, while the teeth of gluttony are rotted away by Diet Pepsi.[17]

The American Eye. Something oddly overlooked in the making of Latin Americanists is that they are to be English-language historians. They can easily pass through graduate school without reading a hun-

dred pages of good English prose. There may be cases of wholesome
stylistic transference between languages—like the influence, we're told,
of Cicero on English parliamentarians. But foreign-language "materials" scanned by the building Latin Americanist seem unlikely to serve
him as a model of economy, precision and suppleness.[18] My own favor-
ites for the purpose are Santayana and Chesterton, who teach that it
takes spirit as well as skill to say what one means.

Style is part of a broader question of outlook. Latin America is
now a semicritical academic specialty subject to progressive subdivi-
sion. Whereas fifteen years ago a Latin Americanist felt himself fortunate to teach one survey course along with assignments in American
or European history, today's market permits even occasional neophytes
to teach exclusively Brazil or Mexico. They foolishly consider this an
intellectual advantage. Specialization is a malady of the times, but
while an obstetrician can probably recognize a case of trachoma or
a severe psychosis, a Brazilianist need never have heard of the Wars of
the Roses or have read Thucydides.

In their new prosperity Latin American studies support a modest
amount of careerism. It takes special gifts and inner drives, however,
for the careerist to satisfy the *Hispanic American Historical Review's*
puritanical canons of specialized research while succumbing to the
blandishments of prestigious publishers for oversynthesized and under-
cooked "teaching materials" (formerly called "books"). An historian's
success story might be traced as follows in an idealized bibliography.
(1) A heavily researched thirty-page article on an obscure Paraguayan
caudillo published in the HAHR, and elsewhere in two Spanish ver-
sions. (2) A monograph on this subject published by an obscure
university press. (3) A well advertised paperback entitled *Hell or
Redemption: An Interpretive Overview of Latin America's Political
Travail from Montezuma to Castro.* This contains chapters cannibal-
ized from several textbooks, a case study of a Paraguayan caudillo, and
a final chapter which treads cautiously between realism and piety,
garnished with quotes from Walt Rostow and Kal Silvert. (4) A paperback anthology entitled *A Reader in Latin American Psychopolitics*
containing the original HAHR article, the final chapter of *Hell or
Redemption,* fifteen articles by colleagues purchased at ludicrously low
permission fees, and two essays translated from Spanish by a graduate
student (gratis).[19] By now our hero has moved from St. Bridget's
o' the Marsh and heads a new Center at Dartnell or the University of

Southwestern Calizona at Pebble Springs. Here his access to funds allows him to shift his research interests and spend two years in Lomas de Chapultepec. The fruit of this sojourn is published in the HAHR as (5) a ten-page article entitled "New Light on the Conquest of Mexico: Pulque Consumption as a Factor in the Military Defeat of the Aztecs." Henceforth his name need appear in print only on rosters of prize committees, in AHA programs as panel chairman, in his graduate students' footnotes, or affixed to prefaces of unmodified "revised" editions of his three books.

Specialization and careerism, whatever private satisfactions they yield, are inadequate models for graduate students, first, because they produce an incoherent, extravagantly eclectic attitude toward the subject of study; second, because they represent alienation from the concerns of the historian's *own* society. Here comes a critical assumption. It is that any historian, even the one lured by distant times or exotic places, functions seriously only when he is writing his way into the pressing moral concerns (which doesn't mean humanitarian or policy concerns) of his immediate situation. The force of Gibbon or Tocqueville or Rostovtzeff resides precisely here. If Latin America remains a satellite speciality in the United States, the fault lies not so much in the parochialism of our national historians as in the failure of Latin Americanists to relate their subject persuasively to their own time and place. A notable exception is Frank Tannenbaum's slender book on slavery which, however tentative and controversial, opened the eyes of a whole platoon of American historians—Elkins, Genovese, Davis, Degler—to the inadequacy of treating slavery in a national perspective. Significantly, Tannenbaum's early studies were of the American South and the American prison system. It may be that the most compelling hypotheses about Latin American history to emanate from our country in the coming decade will be formulated by scholars professionally prepared in the study of United States and not Latin American civilization.

Recommendations are perhaps implicit in what I've said. I'm reluctant to marshal them formally, however, for there's the danger nowadays that someone might thrust half a million dollars into my hand to carry them out. This is because innovation occurring in any obscure corner of our mighty educational establishment is thought to be instantaneously transmissible to all parts of it. Our education system is not even thought of as a network, which at least has transformers and circuit-breakers, but as a giant swimming pool in which a foundation dollar, deposited like a drop of chlorine, will be at work in seconds killing bacteria throughout the tank.

My reticence to prescribe shotgun remedies has also a more immediate source. For the very manner in which Latin Americanists are assembled in history departments militates against the formation of congenial communities of teacher-scholars. They are hired to fill slots on teams. A department boasting an economic historian of modern Mexico endeavors to back him up with a colonial Brazilian church historian. The unity given such a group by the rubric "Latin America" is that of a burlap sack for a peck of potatoes. Competitive faculty recruitment on a "program" basis, brought to fever pitch by current large-scale funding, continually disperses scholars who share similar interests. It acts as an emulsifier on oil slicks of talent. Increasingly we look to conferences, professional meetings and think tanks as the settings for collaboration which campus life now so systematically denies. Boon though it may be to stockholders of Braniff and TWA, this arrangement must be a source of no small mystification to graduate students as their campus programs process them through to degrees in quarantine from the day-to-day conduct of scholarly inquiry.

In this situation any suggestions for improving the education of Latin American historians in scores of graduate departments would have to be revolutionary and perhaps subversive. So I propose an illiberal, perhaps reactionary alternative.[20] Let us establish one or two really first-class institutes, in the old European sense, for the study and teaching of Latin American history. (I doubt if scholars could be found for a larger number.) These wouldn't be pilot projects or experiment stations. They would simply be places where, at long last, one could confidently send gifted graduate students. They would be asylums from the ratrace. They would give us the comfort of saying at home and abroad, "In those two places Latin American history is truly being taught and studied in the United States."

The initiative for creating the centers must come from the historians' guild itself, not from commissars, philanthropoids or praetorian university presidents. The way things are going, I see no reason why the proper task force of historians couldn't simply announce their plans, choose their campuses, write their semiautonomous charters, pick the rosters of scholars, and hand their bill to the various agencies which so beamingly claim to be serving scholarship.

The institute scholars are not to be "Latin Americanists" but historians who know many parts of the world and share consuming interests in some central Latin American themes. Here the working definition of "historian" is someone who believes that the past still lives and must be conjured with. This excludes many professional historians and includes many from other disciplines. The institutes, however, must be devoted to historical rather than interdisciplinary study, for history is by nature transdisciplinary.

And now I close with a confession. After years of interdisciplinary piety I feel constrained to announce, on this most inappropriate occasion, that I find interdisciplinary seminars for the most part a crashing bore, and I'm weary of the elaborate etiquette, disclaimers and private language that obstruct my discourse with economists and literary critics. Polite and tortuous strategies for integrating the disciplines, like those for integrating the races, only exacerbate the original monstrosity of segregation. I see no reason not to proclaim historians to me the *raza cósmica* of Latin American studies.

NOTES   1. At the risk, nay, in the certainty of self-indulgence I list them: "Cultural Differences and Inter-American Relations," *Yale Political*, II, 2 (April 1963): 16, 38–40; "The Strange Career of 'Latin-American Studies,'" American Academy of Political and Social Science, *Annals*, 356 (November 1964): 106–12; "The Two Americas, Musings of a Gringo," *Encounter*, XXV, 3 (September 1965): 90–95; "The Latin American Boom," *The Times Literary Supplement* (July 28, 1966): 683–84; "The Challenge for Foreign Area Studies," The National Association of Secondary-School Principals, *Bulletin*, L, 315 (January 1967): 18–33. Two are laid to rest in anthologies and one, I'm told, found its way into the *Congressional Record*. The only professional virtue I claim for these pieces is their occasional repetitiousness.

2. Arguments of the many who scold me for derogating my colleagues' efforts in literary studies either defend current scholarship or explain why stimulating contributions in the field are not yet possible. One critic, motivated by what I can only call an academic Antigone complex, upholds his fraternity by explaining that one of its principal functions is to give the literary remains of second-rate Latin American authors decent burial with full scholarly apparatus, a courtesy generally denied in the countries of origin.

A symptom of the malady appears in a review in a mass weekly of Carlos Fuentes' latest novel: "Quietly, almost without attracting the attention of our critical sergeants-at-arms, a small group of other Americans has moved in on the American fiction establishment. They come from south of the Rio

Grande. . . ." (*Life,* March 8, 1968). What are our professors of Latin American literature doing, that the invasion of Fuentes, Borges, Cortázar, Guimarães Rosa, Lispector and Vargas Llosa should have occurred so unobtrusively? In fact why aren't some of *our* boys in the American fiction establishment?

3. Our correctives are, like the "problem," culturally conditioned and therefore technologically administered. Just as our answer to school segregation is cross-urban bussing rather than a change in heart, so the answer to rarefied academicism is a massive "program" of intercontinental bussing. The other day a distinguished Latin American visitor confided, "You know, it's *really* a waste of money for you to import me to teach two seminars."

4. The term, I believe, is used by anthropologists, whom I think of as spiritual cousins of historians even though they be self-professed social scientists. For a masterful statement of the cause I defend, however, one would turn to Johan Huizinga's essay "The Task of Cultural History" in *Men and Ideas* (New York, 1959), pp. 17–76.

5. In Seymour Martin Lipset and Aldo Solari, eds., *Elites in Latin America* (New York, 1967), pp. 3–60.

6. On his visit here in the 1920's the historian Huizinga was startled and intrigued to find that the word "behavior" epitomized "the creed of the thinking North American." See his essay "Espíritu norteamericano" in *El concepto de la historia y otros ensayos* (Mexico, 1946), pp. 407–31.

7. Vianna Moog, *Bandeirantes and Pioneers* (New York, 1964), pp. 284–94.

8. Some scholars no longer try to interpret the manifest content of discourse and have resorted to word counts and content analysis.

9. Max Weber, *The Sociology of Religion* (Boston, 1964), pp. 186–90.

10. Fernando Guillén Martínez, "Los Estados Unidos y América Latina," *Aportes,* 7 (Jan. 1968), 4–28. Badly stated, his key proposition is that in the Iberian tradition enjoyment of wealth depends upon prior acquisition of social power, while in ours access to economic opportunity is the precondition for political participation. This contrast has important implications for development, and it orients Latin Americans toward their own historical precedents.

11. Lipset and Solari, pp. 32–33.

12. Nigel Walker, "A New Copernicus?" in Benjamin Nelson, ed., *Freud and the 20th Century* (New York, 1957), p. 24.

13. "I return again and again, in retrospection, to this early untutored interest in books, for how could it have developed, in such isolation and such neglect, but for the presence of some inborn disposition. And faith in such a disposition becomes, with the growth of the personality, a controlling factor. At least, we are only happy so long as our life expands in ever widening circles from the upward gush of our early impulses. . . ." Herbert Read, *The Innocent Eye* (New York, 1947), pp. 49–50.

14. Duberman's experimental seminar, inspired by the writings of A. S. Neill and Paul Goodman and having a bit the air of group therapy, is

described in "An Experiment in Education," *Daedalus* (Winter 1968), 318–41. The thought that the modern professor must become a psychotherapist if his students are not to die of boredom or forever be exploding symptoms does, I admit, depress me.

15. Kenneth Keniston, *The Uncommitted, Alienated Youth in American Society* (New York, 1965).

16. I do not wish to imply that an historian need only cultivate "empathy." His ultimate goal is morphology. Again, Huizinga makes the point: "The true problems of cultural history are always problems of the form, structure, and function of social phenomena. This is not to say that cultural history should be subservient to sociology. Cultural history considers phenomena in their own striking significance, while for sociology they are nothing but paradigms. The cultural historian has abandoned the design of deducing generally valid rules for the knowledge of society from phenomena. He not only sketches the contours of the forms he designs, but colors them by means of intuition and illuminates them with visionary suggestion." *Men and Ideas,* p. 59.

17. I don't know what curricular suggestions all this adds up to. Anyone who interviews students for fellowships knows that they cannot discuss an author unless he has been dished out in "a course." Yet I hesitate to prescribe seminars on Stendhal for all Latin American history students. I sometimes feel that classrooms are as expendable a university landmark as football stadiums.

18. The first version of the only article I ever dared submit to the HAHR came back with the comment that although the subject was interesting my text seemed a literal translation from Portuguese.

19. Latin Americanists now compose their articles with an eye to early anthologization, much as novelists write with the needs of the Hollywood scenarist in mind.

20. My diagnosis of graduate schools seems to agree with that of Christopher Jencks and David Riesman in "Where Graduate Schools Fail," *The Atlantic Monthly* (February 1968): 49–55. They must offer vague, statesmanlike remedies for the larger situation, however, while here I simply treat the grooming of Latin American historians as a *sauve-qui-peut* operation.

Research in Latin America: Problems for the Policy Sciences

CALVIN P. BLAIR

Introduction. Several years ago, Kingsley Davis recounted the hazards and misfortunes which befell those who were engaged in the routine process of taking a population census in India. That particular investigation was met by organized boycott, religious propaganda, superstition, fear, suicide, murder, and even an attack by a tiger.[1] There is a haunting allegory here for those who would prepare investigators for social science research in underdeveloped areas.

To be sure, there are relatively few physical dangers in Latin America these days. And one may assume that any boycott encountered will not likely be organized; that propaganda—religious or otherwise—will be neither more nor less serious a barrier than it might be in the United States; and that any tigers encountered are most likely to be of political stripe. But serious research in the "policy sciences" (defining that term for purposes of this paper to include economics and political science and, by extension, public and business administration) is likely to meet a series of formidable obstacles, including suspicion and fear. It will also meet the difficulties inherent in data that are at once overabundant and very scarce; in the dire shortage of qualified personnel, both North American and Latin American; in methods which promise a great deal more than can be delivered, with inevitable frustrations; and in theories which were never designed to handle the phenomena of rapid economic and social change, and which are frequently difficult or impossible to formulate in useful terms, even for the variables which they *are* meant to handle. As if these were not sufficient deterrents, the North American investigator must wage a continuing struggle to free himself from one of his own culture's most characteristic drives: a strong evangelical or missionary zeal, in this case with reference to economic policy and the "democratic process."

From Camelot to Quandary: Quo vadis, academicus?   In the cleanest of intellectual atmospheres, social science research is neither simple in conception nor clear in purpose. It is no easy matter to convince people to participate voluntarily as good research subjects. Not only in Latin America, but in the world at large, respondents rightly ask themselves what the investigators are up to, anyway. Intellectual curiosity may satisfy the academic, but it takes some persuasion to convince respondents that there are no ulterior motives. Latins are understandably apprehensive when they find themselves under scrutiny, especially by investigators from the United States. The long antagonistic history of U.S.-Latin American relations would be enough to justify a healthy dose of skepticism; but we have more than that. We now have the aftermath of Project Camelot. That fiasco created a real crisis of confidence and shook American social scientists so badly that they began to debate in their inner councils the age-old question of professional ethics and its modern corollary of the relation of the scholar to his government.[2]

The Camelot seed of suspicion fell in fertile soil. We live in an anxious age. The super-states of this world have massive resources for war, large-scale espionage systems, the technology and the temptations for "snooping," and the tactic of cold-war conflict and forestalling which invites intervention in the affairs of smaller and weaker states. The United States, for its part, is in deep trouble; its anxieties are of the kind which can lead to rash action. Thoughtful Latins may wonder whether we won't opt more often for the "safe" policy of intervention. Our role in Guatemala, Cuba, and the Dominican Republic has brought back dramatically the old specter, never far beneath the surface anyway. The art of "understanding" social revolutions has never really advanced as far as that of "controlling" them—where "control" has meant so often "suppression." All of our rhetorical commitment to "peaceful revolution" cannot change our history. Indeed, the very phrase "peaceful revolution" arouses a host of anxieties: from the Right, the worry that we would force a dangerous pace; from the Left, concern that we are merely trying to forestall fundamental changes in the power structure. When our president unveils the world's largest airplane with a speech proclaiming how many troops and how much equipment it will carry how far and how fast, and he adds the warning that this giant new transport machine is but further proof that we will not shrink from the great responsibilities which go with great power, men everywhere may yearn for a clarification of those responsibilities in more careful and more concrete terms.

Subsidies by the C.I.A., even if they had been limited to respectable studies and not doled out for propaganda and political action, would have made all social science research overseas suspect. The glaring contrast between the massive resources devoted to war in Viet Nam, where national purpose has not been convincingly articulated and deep divisions rend the body politic, and the rather meager resources devoted to Latin American development, where so much magnificent rhetoric has led us to believe that the nation is largely of one mind, creates a kind of cynicism on the part of even our friendliest critics. One does not have to be a devoted demonologist to wonder what we are really up to in this world.

"Where goes the United States?" is a question of enormous import to Latin America. More important, for our purposes here, is the question, "Where goes its academic community?" Is it interested in the rest of the world only for purposes of control? Or, though aspiring to scholarly objectivity, does it find itself an unwitting extension of an intelligence system devoted to "national security"? Have social scientists other than the anthropologists proposed that the scholarly community commands a responsibility of higher order than does one's government, except in time of declared war?[3] Do they really mean it? Can they, in fact, hold to such a higher loyalty?

Perhaps this picture of anxiety, suspicion, and fear is overdrawn.

We really do not know. The Latin American Studies Association is planning to take a serious sounding, in selected countries, of the current prospects for social science research in Latin America.

In any event, there are a number of warnings here for the prospective investigator in the policy sciences. First, there is the fact that the source of finance for research is of great importance. Small or obscure foundations are suspect; military and security agencies are out; and even some respectable centers with academic affiliation are tainted. Second, there is the need for careful professional contact; for serious efforts to collaborate with Latin nationals, as often as feasible on *their* initiative; and for institutional ties which will serve Latin American hopes and ambitions, and not merely provide a practice ground for U.S. academics. Third, there is the need to share research results. So often Latin Americans give patiently of their time and ideas in aid of peripatetic scholars from the United States, never to hear of them or their "study" again. It would be a very significant contribution to "understanding" if the best of the studies could be made available in Spanish or Portuguese. Fourth, it would help the general climate of opinion if both the quantity and the quality of debate were raised in academic circles over the responsibilities of the social scientist to the international community of scholars.

Too Much and Too Little: Problems of Personnel and the Information Potpourri. In an excellent review of the state of political science research on Latin America, published just four years ago, Merle Kling used the suggestive analogy of underdevelopment to describe the state of affairs in his discipline.[4] He found investment and returns meager, competent personnel in short supply, technique antiquated, productivity low, innovation almost absent, data grossly inadequate, and systematic analyses scandalously rare.

Kling might well have been speaking for all of the policy sciences. Economics, no less than political science, has been largely an underdeveloped discipline, insofar as the study of Latin America is concerned. Serious research on the area is of recent origin and owes its debts, not primarily to academic scholarship, but rather to a host of international agencies and especially to the Economic Commission for Latin America.[5] It is hardly an exaggeration to say that we know what we do about Latin American economics because of the doctrinal proclivity, the driving desire for empirical knowledge and policy guides, the indefatigable energies, and the ingenious and inventive data-gathering and estimating techniques of ECLA's *técnicos.* The annual *Economic Survey of Latin America,* the *Economic Bulletin for Latin America,* specialized reviews such as *The Economic Development of Latin America in the Post-War Period,*[6] and hundreds of analyses and projections of specific countries, commodities, or industries have poured forth from ECLA to become the substantive information for all who study the area. It is also likely that ECLA's activities have served as a competitive spur to better studies by the Organization of American States. And ECLA's frequent joint efforts with OAS and other bodies are well known.

Because of its reasonably cogent ideological content, which has found the root cause of relative underdevelopment to lie largely in the international trade and investment mechanism, and which proposes major structural changes in Latin American economies, ECLA's output has produced the salutary byproduct effect of forcing even its adversaries to improve their study of the area.

Nevertheless, we know both too much and too little. There is a surfeit of general and descriptive works, isolated in time, place, and focus; and there is an excess of routine data, largely uncoordinated, unevaluated, and of limited use. In economics, too, systematic analytical studies are "scandalously rare," though they are on the increase. Even in the case of rather routine data, there are enormous gaps, so many that the hope of those who would "program" or "plan" are frequently dashed on shoals of ignorance or unavailability. As a case in point, it may be noted that we know next-to-nothing about income distribution in any Latin American country and absolutely nothing in most of them. Even the estimates of income and product, instructed as they are by carefully prepared handbooks and guides, are often built upon rather bold guesses and some relatively simple formula techniques.

The "data gap" may be critical at much lower levels. Much of the simple information needed for economic decisions does not exist, as anyone can testify who has attempted an investment survey, a market study, a family income survey, or any of a host of other studies. The critical role of a well-designed census, carefully taken and promptly published, can hardly be exaggerated. Yet in much of Latin America there is long delay in the publication of census results. As examples, one might cite the population census taken in the Dominican Republic in 1960, for which much of the information is still not published; or the industrial census of 1958 taken in Guatemala, published for the first time six years later.

The faults do not all lie in official agencies or on the other side of the border. College professors too (including the writer) are sometimes inordinately slow in publishing the results of their own investigations, despite their tantalizing descriptions of forthcoming attractions which one encounters in the *Latin American Research Review*.

On the Latin American side, there is great need for the promotion of basic social science research. Outside of a few stellar institutions such as the Instituto Torcuato di Tella in Argentina, the Fundacão Getulio Vargas in Brazil, the Instituto de Economía in Chile, and El Colegio de México, virtually all economic and social analysis is done by government agencies or official international bodies who attack specific problems with which they have been charged by the political systems which they serve.

In part, the problem of "detached" research is one of a shortage of trained personnel. Very few Latin Americans are able to give their full time to research, and perhaps their societies could scarcely afford the luxury of scholarly devotion. I can't speak for the political scientists, because I don't really know how many exist or what they do; but every Latin American economist whom I have known has been engaged in the equivalent of three full-time jobs. The demand for *técnicos* in government and the international agencies is so great throughout Latin America that there is little talent left over for more than part-time teaching and research. We have the anomaly that those whose experience has provided them with perhaps the most important questions for study are too involved in terms of both time-commitment and policy-commitment to be free for much in the way of "scholarly" research. The profession of economist in Latin America is an eminently practical one, in a way which has never been true in the United States. That is on the whole a good thing; but it is bad for the present and the future of basic social science research.

Method and Theory: Overreach, Undergrasp, and Some Signs of the Times. It is not only Latin America that is in transition. So, too, are the social sciences whose methods and theoretical structures are to provide us with the framework for viewing that process of change.

The refinement of statistical techniques, the proliferation of record-keeping of various sorts (especially that associated with collection of taxes), the advent of the tape recorder and the electronic computer—all have greatly increased our abilities to gather and to manipulate information. They have also increased our capacity for deception.

The earliest and easiest of the techniques for deceiving one another is to give fancy new names to old processes or subject matter. In contemporary jargon, for example, "specifying the variables" may mean only listing the things which interest you; "business communication" may refer simply to letter-writing; "management science" or "organizational theory" may mean merely the orderly discussion of ways in which humans react to one another; a "matrix" may be just another table; "behavioral science" may be another label for anthropology or psychology; "oral history" may mean just interviews; and "model-building" may mean something as simple as the writing of an equation. Each of these terms can, however, imply more than new names; and they often imply an increased effort at measurement, quantification, manipulation of data, specification of relationships, simulation, and generalization of results.

Computers are here to stay. Their enormous capacity and speed in routine calculations and data processing make them a godsend for certain types of analysis; and they offer suggestive and stimulating, if not always fruitful, possibilities for "experimenting" with symbolic and analog models. Students of the social sciences from this point forward are sure to use them as routinely as older generations used the typewriter or the desk calculator. All is not net gain, however. The drudgery that once went into tabulation, calculation of correlation coefficients, or the decomposition of times series may have been wiped out by program libraries of solution routines. But in its stead comes the time and energy which must be spent in learning programming languages and the routines of button-pushing. Schools everywhere seem bent, in this infatuation stage, on requiring large numbers of students to learn the mechanics of the new trade, just as they once required everyone to learn to type (a practice now largely abandoned).

There are other dangers. Good theory precedes good calculation. It is almost inevitable, in our rush to build "science," that our quantitative reach far exceeds our grasp. Many relationships must be arbitrarily quantified for manipulation in computer models, even when our good sense tells us that the very notion of quantity may be inappropriate. And the subtleties and complexities of real human systems often defy the model-builder—to say nothing of the paucity of data referred to above. For example, both the necessary information and the necessary theory are currently insufficient for comprehensive model-building for Latin American planning or integration, however pressing the political or economic need in either case. To take quite a different example, some cultural forms, like peasant agriculture or the Viet Cong, have incredible survival value, despite our computerized efforts to deal with them.

There remains the embarrassing question of the relevance of contemporary theory. Good theory yields better theory, it is true; but really good theory also yields useful results. Plane geometry is good theory not only because of its internal logic and beauty and the string of theorems which it offers up, but also because it has been of great use to navigators, surveyors, and architects.

On the score of utility, much of the theoretical apparatus of the policy sciences scores rather low. I am not equipped to add a mot to Kling's eloquent review of the defects of political science,[7] except to note that things *are* changing in some of the ways which he indicated were needed. Even economics, long thought to have a higher claim to the label of science, is riddled with ideology and replete with concepts without specifiable dimensions or without hope of meaningful estimates. Micro-economics was headed into many a non-utilitarian dead end until linear programming and the injection of new behavioral notions set it off in what may prove to be fruitful directions. Lest I be thought to exaggerate, consider, as an example, how difficult it is to estimate price or income elasticities of demand for any given commodity. We learn from the abundant literature that too many things change at once, that the necessary data are too difficult or too expensive to get, that the statistical estimating techniques tend to bias the answers, and that the quantitative estimates which we do obtain may be valid only for historically unique circumstances.[8] Contrast that state of affairs with the physical sciences, where concepts have been defined and techniques developed in such ways as to fill large volumes with tables of critical constants or measures which can be obtained repeatedly by independent investigators.

This is not to argue that economics is "unscientific" or that its concepts are useless, but merely to argue the obvious point that economic theory often is not very good theory when "good" means "useful," which it must surely mean. We may note in passing that the same could be said, not so long ago, of much of physical science theory as well.

Economists still cling to the beauty of internal logical consistency and deductive theory, and they still tend to "quote scripture" where they cannot adduce evidence (i.e., they often give "authoritative" rather than "experimentally convincing" answers). When it comes to the phenomena of development, we simply haven't created a very useful body of theory yet, though there is abundant doctrine of varied kind. I shall here revert to the form which I just described by citing two authors who agree with me. Carlos Massad, in reviewing the state of economic research in Latin America, observed that economic analysis is used to promote a particular view of the world, that the tools of analysis are rather unsatisfactory for tackling the problems of growth, and that Latin American economists are under "strong pressures to answer questions they are not prepared to answer."[9] Dudley Seers has offered a similar observation:

> If there was ever a time when one could see a major revolution in doctrine looming ahead, it is today. And the reasons are, as always, because the existing body of theory cannot explain what has to be explained, nor can it give the help that is politically essential.[10]

One of the signs of our time of transition is to be found in hasty efforts to calm an identity crisis in the social science professions. Those of us over forty can attempt a bit of retreading by attending conferences on "explanatory theory" (I didn't know there was any other kind of theory—but a conference for political scientists was held under precisely that title just recently at my home university). Or perhaps we can enroll for eight weeks in the Inter-University Consortium seminars on research design, data analysis, mathematical political analysis, or quantitative methods in history.

Conclusion: Call off the Missionaries. Given the state of the art, one would think that theorists and practitioners in the policy sciences would be humble about offering advice. But just the opposite is the case. On both sides of the border, prescription is largely unhindered by analysis. And many kinds of representatives of U.S. culture are evangelical in their zeal to prescribe for Latin America.

Businessmen are perhaps the worst offenders, understandably so, given their vested interests and their play to the United States government (rather than to Latin America) as their real audience. The Commerce Committee for the Alliance for Progress, a star-studded group of 25 very big U.S. businessmen, presented the Department of Commerce a report, early in 1963, containing the following gem:

> Our proposals will be insufficient to complete the task unless the philosophy of economic liberty and equal opportunity which is the basis of the free enterprise system, and which has developed the United States to its present greatness, is brought to bear in every aspect of economic, social, and political life in Latin America.[11]

No committee has either the knowledge or the analytical skill to reach such a policy conclusion. It was sheer soap-box oratory.

The academic profession is not exempt from like behavior. Consider the study written by a respectable political scientist, with lots of experience in Latin America, on the theme of private enterprise.[12] His recommendations at the ends of chapters urge Latin businessmen to adopt competition, efficiency, modern management, and a host of other U.S. norms, including the transfer of government-owned firms to the private sector.

Latin American history also has its many examples of economic advisory missions from the United States, some of them seemingly eager to install in the host country some ideal held dear but unattained back home.[13]

It is not only businessmen, academics, or the National Planning Association who are overtly missionary. The Peace Corps, AID, the Ford Foundation, private charity groups—all have a common drive to "help" by "showing the way." Now, there may be a small role for foreign missionaries in Latin America, especially for those who are prepared to give out large sums of money. But it is incredibly arrogant to assume either that we usually know the way or that Latins are eager to follow the way as we see it.

For social science investigators, at the very least, the question about Latin America must be, "What have we here, and how does it work?" not "How can we change it?"

NOTES 1. Kingsley Davis, *The Population of India and Pakistan* (Princeton: Princeton University Press, 1951), p. 5; as reported in Herbert H. Hyman, "Research Design," in Robert E. Ward *et al.*, *Studying Politics Abroad* (Boston: Little, Brown and Company, 1964), pp. 154–55.

2. The Camelot question was treated with sensitivity by Kalman H. Silvert in "American Academic Ethics and Social Research Abroad," American Universities Field Staff, *West Coast-South America Series*, XII, 3 (1965). Richard N. Adams has discussed the question of professional ethics and the role of the scholar, with special reference to anthropologists, in "Ethics and the Social Anthropologist in Latin America," *American Behavioral Scientist*, X, 10 (June 1967): 16–21.

3. See Adams, *op. cit.*, 19.

4. Merle Kling, "The State of Research on Latin America: Political Science," in Charles Wagley, ed., *Social Science Research on Latin America* (New York: Columbia University Press, 1964): pp. 168–213.

5. See Carlos Massad, "Economic Research in Latin America," in Charles Wagely, ed., *Social Science Research on Latin America*, pp. 214–42.

6. Economic Commission for Latin America, *The Economic Development of Latin America in the Post-War Period* (New York: United Nations, Sales No.: 64.II G.6, 1964).

7. Kling, *op. cit.*

8. See the discussions in Robert Brown, *Explanation in Social Science* (Chicago: Aldine Publishing Company, 1963); and in Paul H. Rigby, *Conceptual Foundations of Business Research* (New York: John Wiley and Sons, Inc., 1965).

9. Massad, *op. cit.*, pp. 214–15.

10. Dudley Seers, "Limitations of the Special Case" in Kurt Martin and John Knapp, eds., *The Teaching of Development Economics* (Chicago: Aldine Publishing Company, 1967), p. 2.

11. "Proposals to Improve the Flow of U.S. Private Investment to Latin America," Report of the Commerce Committee for the Alliance for Progress, 1963. Reprinted in *Private Investment in Latin America,* Hearings Before the Sub-committee on Inter-American Economic Relationships of the Joint Economic Committee, Congress of the United States, 88th Congress, 2nd Session (Washington: U.S. Government Printing Office, 1964), p. 57.

12. Frank Brandenburg, *The Development of Latin American Private Enterprise,* Planning Pamphlet No. 121 (Washington: National Planning Association, 1964).

13. See Albert O. Hirschman, "Inflation in Chile," in *Journeys Toward Progress: Studies of Economic Policy-Making in Latin America* (New York: The Twentieth Century Fund, 1963), p. 168.

Preparing the Investigator in Literature

FRANK DAUSTER

I was pleased to note on the program for today's discussion that I represent something called "literature," rather than an even more amorphous and indefinable entity called "language" or "Spanish" or even "Lusohispanic." These are all terms which lump together a series of strange bedfellows indeed, and before presuming to make some comments on the problems involved in preparing the investigator, it might be advisable to determine just which investigator we wish to prepare. In other words, what is the discipline to which we must address ourselves, and what are its special characteristics and problems?

It seems to me that there are rather greater differences of specialization within the area of "language and literature" than might be suspected. The doctorate in Spanish or Portuguese may mean that the holder is a philologist in the classical sense, a man widely learned in the complex interrelationships between language and its capacity for esthetic expression. He may be a linguist, tangentially interested, if at all, in literature or what we presume to call culture, perfectly capable of functioning professionally without any special reference to a literary subject matter. Assuming, however, that our hypothetical scholar is primarily interested in literature in Spanish or Portuguese, his specialty may range from medieval literature of the Peninsula to the recent novels of Brazil or Spanish America. And let it not be thought that I exaggerate the degree or kind of specialization. The nature and problems of professional literary scholarship vary enormously according to the nature of the specialization, and the tools required are often markedly different. Further, the bulk of published material is such that the scholar almost perforce retreats into a small corner of research. The specialist in medieval Spanish literature is unable to function without Latin and German, and it is increasingly obvious that a thorough knowledge of Arabic and Hebrew are indispensable in certain areas, in addition to the normal battery of Catalán, Provençal, Italian, Portuguese and French. The Latin Americanist, unless he be a student of early Colonial literature, has no need for such esoteric equipment; Portuguese and French provide him with the linguistic tools necessary. The medievalist is far too occupied with the broad range of medieval European literature and the acquisition of his language skills to have time for the Brazilian novel; the Latin Americanist must cope with the literary output of most of our hemisphere, and he has neither the time nor the inclination to attempt to handle much more.

Yet, in general terms, whatever the discipline closest to the heart of our potential scholar, we find that he is subject to the same basic program of training, to the same pattern of graduate courses, language competence tests and graduate examinations. It is hardly feasible, and manifestly not desirable, to be trained exclusively in contemporary Latin American fiction or 15th Century Spanish poetry. No scholar worth his salt can afford to be ignorant of the background of the literature and the culture which has helped form the matrix of the literature to whose study he will devote his professional life. To approach the professional study of Mario Vargas Llosa without knowing the *Quixote* is ludicrous; to devote oneself to the Peruvian satirical tradition of Colonial poetry without a solid grounding in Golden Age Spanish satire is folly.

But an extraordinary amount of literature has been written in Spanish since it first differentiated itself from Latin. In practical terms, what may be considered a proper, just and balanced preparation for the potential scholar? Ideally, this would appear a relatively simple matter. As Robert Mead has admirably stated, "No student specializing in 'Spanish' (or 'Portuguese') should receive even an A.B. degree unless he is adequately grounded in the history, language, culture and contemporary life of *both* the Peninsula and the New World."[1] Leaving aside for a moment the matters of culture and contemporary life, as well as the sheer feasibility of such a program, and restricting ourselves entirely to the question of literature, the ideal statement we have just heard is simply not a reflection of practice. In most universities it is difficult, if not impossible, to avoid a program of formal courses and a series of doctoral examinations which are rather heavily oriented toward Peninsular literature. Admittedly, many universities now have a program of options, but it is still possible to receive the doctorate in "Spanish" without ever having read a Latin American work. Obviously, the reverse is not true, nor would I wish it to be so. To pretend, however, that such a program reflects the reality of literature in Spanish is arrant nonsense.

To what do we owe this lamentable situation? Latin American literature is a very new field. As late as 1921, Alfred Coester, in many sense the dean of studies of Spanish American literature in the United States, could write, "As to the originality of Spanish-American literature it lies chiefly in the subject-matter, in its picture of natural scenery and social life."[2] A few sentences later, we learn that "the reader, aware at the outset that he has before him an extremely provincial type of literature, will not expect great masterpieces."[3] It is worth noting that this remarkably defensive statement appeared decades after the *Modernista* movement had effected a radical alteration in literature in Spanish.

Such a short-sighted approach to the whole question of Latin American literature might well appear to be ancient history. Unfortunately, such is not the case. As recently as Dec. 30, 1965, Professor Mead felt the need to call for a final end to "la nefasta y sorda guerra entre los peninsulares y los criollos. Hacer que en nuestros programas de enseñanza se reconozca la paridad entre los valores culturales de la península ibérica y los de los países de América, y hacer que se declare que el único hispanista verdadero es el que conozca, estime y sepa interpretar ambas culturas."[4] Lest these strong words be dismissed lightly, it should be noted that they were delivered as part of the

Presidential Address of the American Association of Teachers in Spanish and Portuguese. The fact that such a statement was felt to be necessary and addressed to the professional organization for all teachers of Spanish and Portuguese certainly underlines the gravity of the problem.

What are the implications of this "silent war" for our hypothetical investigator? If I may be permitted to quote Professor Mead a bit further, he states that ". . . the interests of a majority of the students . . . orient them toward Iberoamérica . . ." while ". . . the interests and training of a majority of their instructors orient them towards Spain and Portugal."[5] Approximately 70% of the teachers of Spanish in the United States are Peninsular oriented.[6] The simple fact is that the structure of our graduate programs is determined in many cases by a staff which has undergone little, if any, training in Latin American literature, which knows little about it, and which, however well-intentioned, continues to reflect the paternalistic attitude expressed by Coester forty-seven years ago.

The upshot is that the fledgling Latin Americanist knows rather less about Latin American literature than he should, rather more about Spanish literature than he needs, and almost nothing about other areas of vital import to him. Which leads to the second problem of definition of discipline which faces us today. It is entirely possible that our potential scholar may be interested exclusively in close textual analysis or that he may be inclined toward sociological criticism; what is certain is that he will, for the first years of his professional life, earn his bread by the teaching of language. The control of Spanish or Portuguese will not be a research tool but a necessity. However gifted as a research scholar, if he does not speak at least one of these languages with near-native facility and accent, he will have considerable difficulty in entering the profession.

Our potential scholar, then, is faced with the double task of mastering a complex subject field and of attaining near-native linguistic competency. In practical terms, the latter means that he must spend a considerable part of his undergraduate training in the study of language *per se,* and that the courses in literature will not be able to cover as much material as would comparable courses in a department of English. It is perfectly obvious that the undergraduate, however capable and motivated, cannot read with the same facility in the language he is studying. The massive problem of sheer bulk of material already discussed is then aggravated by the fact that the language problems almost inevitably prevent the student from having achieved the same level of subject-matter familiarity which may reasonably be expected of potential scholars who need not concern themselves with authenticity of intonation and whose training and reading are, generally, in their native tongue.

The final question of disciplinary definition which faces us today has to do with professional specialization. Our potential scholar must needs wear three hats; he is simultaneously a Spanish teacher, a Hispanist in the broad sense, and a Latin Americanist, which adds still a further dimension to his already discouraging problem. If he were a specialist in close textual analysis or in literary history of the sort which regards extraliterary factors as of no major import, he would be perfectly well off within the traditional structure of our graduate schools. He would, however, be a Latin Americanist much as he might be a descriptive linguist or a botanist, capable of being transported anywhere and simply applying his techniques to whatever flora, dialect or poem happened to be close to hand.

But this is not the potential Latin Americanist to whom this group addresses itself. Presumably, we are concerned about the future scholar who is alert to his world, who is committed to the study of Latin America today. In short, to the man who fits Professor Mead's description of the ideal Hispanist, and whose professional commitment is to the turbulent and fascinating literature of Latin America. He is, indeed, a man who will face almost insuperable obstacles. In addition to being held responsible at some time in his career for a mass of material which will seem to him irrelevant—and which, in many cases, will be just as irrelevant as it seems—in addition to the labor of love necessary to master his language, he will be faced, as he enters his profession, with filling an enormous gap in his professional equipment. He cannot function without familiarity with pertinent materials from all fields of study. Few literary critics, and certainly no Latin Americanist worthy of the name, can possibly function without a broad awareness of the phenomena normally lumped under the jurisdiction of the social sciences. I wish to be completely clear; I do not refer to the disguised sociologist who is interested exclusively in the novel as a source of raw material for studies of social mobility or family tensions, and whose contributions to the professional literature will add nothing to literary criticism and precious little to sociology. I refer to the scholar for whom Carlos Fuentes, to take one example, is a novelist of some stature, and who is absorbed in questions of Fuentes' technical capacities, with the lucid and important insights into the fabric of Mexico which Fuentes' works provide, and with the complex interrelationships between form and content without which the novels may not be understood properly. Such a scholar must be reasonably acquainted with history, with sociology and anthropology and economics. At a time when Latin American literature is committed to its own world as perhaps never before, when it is in the most literal sense an image of its own world, the proper apprehension and appreciation of that world and that literature require a truly formidable preparation. Equally important, they require that we have more than a casual awareness of our own world. We can little appreciate or understand what is significant and distinct about Latin America unless we know ourselves.

But where and when are we to lay the groundwork for this complex apprehension? Certainly, not in the normal program of the normal doctorate. There is simply no time. The picture becomes even more depressing when we realize how few potential scholars finish their degrees, due in some measure, I suspect, to the factors we have been discussing. In a recent issue of *Ventures,* the publication of the Yale Graduate School, John Perry Miller refers to Rosenhaupt's study of the experience at Columbia, where the average length of time required to complete the Ph.D. in the humanities was 9.4 years, as compared to 8.9 years in the social sciences and 6 in the physical sciences.[7] That is, it takes more than half again as long in the humanities as in the sciences. This depressing statistic is accompanied by a chart indicating that of all candidates for the degree enrolled at Yale during the period 1955–1959, only 60% had completed the degrees by June, 1966.

It is obvious that the obstacles to receipt of the degree are sufficient unto themselves, without further complications. Dean Miller summarizes the problem:

> The criticisms and prescriptions have been many. Some would change the basic nature of the Ph.D. as a research degree. Some, noting that the degree has become the union card for college teaching, question the appropriateness of the typical research program for such careers. Some have been critical of the nature of dissertation research, especially but not solely in the humanities. Some urge that topics chosen should be narrower and dissertations shorter. Some urge that students concern themselves with broader problems of interpretation and synthesis, but even they have generally urged that such topics be treated at shorter length. For many, of course, the problem seems to be one

of supply. Their principal concern is simply that there are so few new Ph.D.'s to be hired! But, the one consistent theme upon which both the defenders of the establishment and its critics are agreed is that the rate of drop-out is too great and the stretch-out on the way to the degree too long. Something funny happens in the academic procession on the way from matriculation to commencement. So few of those who matriculate remain "to commence," and among those who do "commence" too many have become too old and too tired.[8]

It is not my purpose to enter this already heated discussion of what is wrong with our doctoral programs, except insofar as it has a bearing on our subject here today. It is apparent that I have been critical of the existing programs for rather opposite reasons than those mentioned by Dean Miller. I am convinced that our present programs do not do an adequate job of training potential scholars of Latin American literature. I hasten to add that I am completely in sympathy with Dean Miller's remarks, and with many of the suggestions enunciated by the numerous articulate critics of the system. Many of the reforms already initiated at various institutions are far overdue, and such programs as area studies are certainly a step in the proper direction. But I question whether they truly answer the problem. The scholar is a man trained in a discipline, equipped to investigate the complex spectrum of problems which occur within that discipline. I am not at all sure that a broad area program without a firm disciplinary base will produce much more than rather confused young people who do not have a solid disciplinary grounding in anything. In the words of James Thorpe, "Although the scholar's great adversary is ignorance, his great adversity is confusion."[9] Of some things, however, I am very certain. From 1949 to 1963, 69% of all completed doctorates in Lusohispanic letters were in peninsular Spanish literature, 27% in Spanish American Literature, and 4% in Lusobrazilian. In cold figures, the period 1962–1964 produced 53 new Ph.D.'s in Spanish American literature, as opposed to 105 in peninsular literature. These figures represent substantially less than one-half of the number listed as in progress for the same three-year period, and even allowing for a general increase in enrollments, it seems obvious that the percentage of degrees actually completed in Spanish around the country is substantially less than the 60% for Yale.[10]

It seems clear from all the foregoing that despite the attraction which Latin America exerts on potential scholars, the actual production of properly trained investigators is subject to powerful negative pressures. The present system for preparing these investigators answers neither their needs nor those of the profession. It is a system which lies withering under what William Arrowsmith has so justly called the dead hand of the past.[11] It seems to me that the first order of business is to remove this dead hand and to breathe life and relevance into a training program in order that it produce investigators properly equipped to deal with their field.

NOTES   1. "Canto de cisne: The AATSP Today and Tomorrow," *Hispania,* XLV, 4 (December 1962): 736.

2. *The Literary History of Spanish America* (New York: The Macmillan Company, 1921), p. ix.

3. *Op. cit.,* p. x.

4. ". . . the ill-omened and unvoiced war between peninsulars and creoles. To see to it that in our teaching programs parity between the cultural values of the Iberian Peninsula and those of the countries of America should be recognized and that it should be proclaimed that the only true Hispanist is he who is acquainted with, esteems and knows how to interpret both cultures." (Editor's translation)
"La enseñanza del español y del portugués en los Estados Unidos: Anhelos y realidades," *Hispania,* XLIX 1 (March 1966): 20–21.

5. "Canto de cisne," 736.

6. "La literatura iberoamericana en los EE UU: Tergiversación de una polémica," *Cuadernos Americanos,* CXLIII, 6 (November–December 1965): 139.

7. *Ventures* (Fall 1967): 2.

8. *Op. cit.,* 1.

9. "Introduction," *The Aims and Methods of Scholarship in Modern Languages and Literatures* (New York: Modern Language Association, 1963), p. ix.

10. The sources for these figures are the annual listings in *Hispania,* and especially William J. Smither's "Dissertations in the Hispanic Languages and Literatures-1963," *Hispania,* XLVII, 2 (May 1964): 326.

11. "The Shame of the Graduate Schools," *Harper's* (March 1966): 51–59.

Commentary*

HOWARD F. CLINE   The stated topic of this session was "Preparing the investigator for a changing hemisphere." I propose to follow the precedent set by our four distinguished speakers by ignoring it completely, and to unburden myself of remarks on the "human condition" as manifested in academia. About the only common strand I have been able to trace through the previous presentations is that the situation seems deplorable, in a variety of ways and for sundry reasons, most of them beyond the capability of the group here to remedy.

It surely must be discouraging for students, and younger persons who are trying to prepare students to investigate a changing hemisphere, to learn of the formidable obstacles ahead of them, the pitfalls into which they may unwittingly stumble, and the hazards they must face abroad and at home. However, I have a message of cheer: if students irrationally persist in becoming

---

* The author has revised his commentary for publication. The revisions include the addition of extended remarks on Project Camelot.—Ed.

scholars by hard work, skill, or the academic craftiness which Dr. Morse has so delightfully documented, the rewards are great. Three or four books, fifty articles, and several hundred book reviews later they may look forward to providing commentary on four excellent, but otherwise unrelated papers by highly esteemed colleagues.

Alphabetically, and in order of the presentations, the remarks by Dr. Adams first are scrutinized here by a hopefully impartial eye. Perhaps an initial statement is that many of the trends and phenomena he describes for behavioral science research in and about Latin America are by no means unique or exclusive to it, but rather are generalized for similar undertakings in other world areas, and more especially in the so-called underdeveloped or emerging nation areas. Wherever charges of U.S. political imperialism are heard frequently and believed widely by the intellectual and political elite, charges of U.S. academic mercantilism and scholarly imperialism are seldom absent, and characteristically the suspicion that the roving U.S. investigator is probably a spy forms part of the stereotype. This is merely to say that the young student who may wish to avoid some of the problems Dr. Blair posed in Latin America for him by shifting to African, Asian, or Soviet studies will face much the same general situation. In fact, in comparison Latin America is less bleak: most African nations prescribe, within very narrow limits, what can be researched in their lands by "colonial imperialists." India, Egypt, the Soviet Union, and mainland China as an extreme case, to mention merely a few examples among dozens of places, have similar proscriptive rules, all generally more restrictive than any found in Latin America.

However, there exists in Latin America, as elsewhere, and presumably there will continue to exist a very large reality, one that Dr. Adams deplores. In discussing the desirability of having the national research needs of Latin American countries placed in some rational order of priorities on which national science policies could be based, he notes that "scientific activity dictated solely by non-scientific concerns will, over the long run, weaken science as a whole." I think the prospective researcher should begin to live as early as possible with the fact that national policies, whether for government, economics, or science, are set by political leaders, not by technicians, and normally are directed towards achieving what seems to them to be the national interest. Seldom does this include the abstract universe which is peopled in part by what Adams has called the supra-disciplinary types, those mystical beings who are "not concerned with subject matter as it has been defined in the classical disciplines, but with any series of human behaviors that can be subjected to analyses of the variety being devised in the abstract." As I do not think that within the foreseeable future the political climates in the several Latin American countries will shift markedly, I would stress paying close attention to Dr. Adams' final remarks on the constraints which these conditions impose so far as choice of topics, study site, and other elements of a research design are concerned.

Perhaps one of the most traumatic experiences a young student must undergo is to learn, either the hard way by running into blank walls or even jails or through discussions with his elders (i.e., dodderers over the age of 30) that some topics, however intrinsically interesting to him and even his mentors, are closely unresearchable in the present imperfect universe. This was brought vividly home to me not long ago when a young graduate student, who had perfected his grantsmanship skills to the point of obtaining support for two or three years in Spain, came to seek advice on how he should go about learning the way the *guardia civil* in Spain really operated. Only two of these portly but lethal gentlemen are needed to keep law and order in any Spanish town, and their office is nearly hereditary. Although I suggested that an investigation of the Mafia in Sicily would perhaps impose less likelihood of negative results he would not settle for that safer topic. I have not heard from him recently.

Professor Blair reaffirms that the Age of Aquarius even pervades academia, that anxieties, uncertainties, the crumbling of hallowed verities that haunt the world are by no means absent from the policy sciences in relation to research on Latin America. Independently he reiterates and corroborates matters also touched by Dr. Adams, notably in his opening statements. Moreover, Dr. Blair makes explicit some matters implicit in the Adams treatment.

Mature students of all ages are continually concerned with what he calls "the age-old question of professional ethics and its modern corollary of the relation of the scholar to his government." Quite wisely, I believe, he poses, without attempting even tentative answers, basic questions in his extension of his query, "Where is [the United States's] academic community going?" The whole matter of allegiances and loyalties is a vexing, complicated, emotion-laden topic. Dr. Blair asks if social scientists other than anthropologists have gone on record as affirming that the scholarly community commands a responsibility of higher order than does one's government, except in time of declared war.

So far as I am familiar with the literature, the answer is no. It should be added that in both the social and behavioral, or policy sciences (the terminology is as confused as some of their views) and in the humanities there is polarization among scholars along political lines. Younger men (or those who would like to be thought so) with high moral fervor have increasingly and vocally questioned authority—that of their elders, their academic institutions, their academic guilds, their national government. The political action and activism which once was thought to be a somewhat aberrant trait of Latin American university students has not only obviously spread to students on American campuses, but to faculties as well. Confrontation politics has made appearance at the hitherto staid, usually dull, business meetings of learned societies and professional associations. Thus to the politicizing of research noted by Dr. Adams should be added an element of radicalizing.

Dr. Blair asks, in relation to the anthropologists' appeal to some higher moral plane for denying their first allegiance to their country and replacing it with an ill-defined and amorphous scientific community, "Do they really mean it? Can they, in fact, hold to such a higher loyalty?" We can only echo his answer about other matters: "We really do not know."

Social and behavioral scientists have not told us very much about how social and behavioral scientists behave. They have not provided analyses or models of how much the writer is the politicized animal, how much the scientist, how much the emotional being when writing about topics that may involve such elements. I think I would agree with Dr. Adams that these variables would not necessarily all come into play when the scientist is primarily concerned with preceramic lithic industries or linguistic change, but they certainly all seem to emerge when any one of them writes about Camelot.

For a moment I should like to digress and tell you something about that ill-starred venture. I speak with a certain knowledge, although now with no particular authority, as one of the scholarly group which the National Research Council named in the early stages of that venture to advise it and the Army Research Office concerning Project Camelot. I should add that apparently we were capable enough sci-

entists to predict rather accurately what would happen if certain proposals and approaches were not modified to meet the obvious moral
and professional requirements of the U.S. and Latin American research
communities, and that when such basic modification of approach was
not forthcoming, we resigned. Unfortunately our dire predictions came
true.

Among the recommendations thus early voiced was that, at the first
opportunity, responsible social scientists in Latin America be ap-
praised of the nature and aims of the project and should be involved
in the development of its design. A second major recommendation was
that sponsorship of the project should be shifted from the transparent
"academic" cover employed by the Army to a respectable and overt
independent sponsorship by the Smithsonian Institution or similar
autonomous administrative organ whose scientific integrity has been
unquestioned. Coupled with this were recommendations that all findings should remain unclassified and publicly available. Without avail
we also tried to have the peculiar jargon employed by the Pentagon re-
placed by perhaps equally peculiar but more familiar social "sciencese."

The latter was more than a minor quarrel over semantics. Camelot
was to be a very elaborate study of what in military terminology they
like to call "counter-insurgency." This obviously conjures up to the lay
mind evil images of the movement of tanks and battle-dressed units
to wipe out idealistic rebels against the Establishment. In this instance,
however, what they were really talking about, they said, was "nation-
binding," an identification of variables and their interrelationships in
changing societies. A simple illustration would be an effort to identify
which elements seemed more significant to restive villagers: schools,
roads, sanitation, religion, or a great number of other possibilities.
Armed with this knowledge, the purpose would be to respond to symptoms of restiveness by meeting the most pressing needs through civic,
rather than military, action and thereby prevent insurgency. Thus as
a total design the Camelot project had as its long-term aim the study
in depth of one functioning Latin American society, as a whole, bringing to bear a large battery of social and behavioral science techniques.
This is the sort of enterprise which Dr. Adams has noted a single
scholar cannot undertake alone, and even a small team could provide
only minimal or partial results. The concept, therefore, was to bring
together a large multidisciplinary team with adequate funding. This
seems wholly legitimate.

At an early inter-agency meeting the non-government social scientists on the advisory panel were apparently astounded to hear the Deputy Director of Research for the Central Intelligence Agency state that the Camelot project should be absolutely overt, be under respectable scholarly auspices, and that its results be made available in orthodox published form. He added that even if the Agency had data that might be relevant, its participation might seriously taint the undertaking. Accustomed as most scholars are to conceive of the CIA in comic-book stereotypes and generally ill-informed of its basic organization into operations and evaluation units (with perhaps 90% of the information for the latter coming from published materials) some of the academics present still thought there might be something specious in these statements. However, so far as I know (as Deputy Chairman of the NRC panel, with relatively high security clearances) the CIA thereafter had no further contact with Project Camelot. Its continued position was that anything that came out of the project in published form would be sufficient grist for the CIA mill.

Let me elaborate slightly a point merely touched on by Dr. Adams, who correctly states that the Army Research Office moved into a vacuum caused by the decline in quantity and quality of social science investigations earlier undertaken, with some notable successes, by the Department of State. Congress and the Secretaries of State (the non-scientists who run our affairs) steadily downgraded External Research in State which in a happier day could and possibly would have undertaken Camelot perhaps in conjunction with the Smithsonian Institution. About $6 million in research funds were committed by the Army for Camelot, more money than External Research had available for all its activities over a decade. With certain bureaucratic logic, and perhaps not a little cupidity, it was the view of the people at External Research that such research involved foreign areas for which State had responsibility, and that the funds should channel through their agency. The intra-Departmental tussle went on: Army moved Camelot from its service level to a Defense Department project, while External Research similarly internally escalated the problem to the point that at Cabinet level McNamara faced Rusk, and it was up to the President to decide who would oversee or administer social science research in foreign areas carried out on appropriated U.S. Federal funds.

The President decided in favor of Rusk, but did not order transfer of funds to carry out Project Camelot. By then the public hue and cry about it had made a dead duck of the project. But the decision has left a legacy. An office in the Department of State continues under Presidential fiat to review all research proposals from executive agencies which directly involve social science research abroad employing Federal funding. I am not privy to its operations and I am hesitant to say more about the matter than to state that to date I have heard few if any complaints about its actions, from within or from outside the Government.

One of the aspects of the whole Camelot affair which does cause personal scholarly concern is how quickly piecemeal, partial, and often incomplete if not incorrect information and figments about it became articles of faith for scholars talking and writing about Camelot. So far as I know, none of them has employed his famed interview techniques with some of the major planning participants; few if any have apparently delved into the public records such as those of the National Research Council advisory panel meetings, or have gone very far beyond rehashing some of the early published accounts, themselves based often on wildly distorted newspaper coverage. Perhaps the Camelot episode has receded far enough into history to permit a responsible group of scientists, acting as scientists, to establish a little more objective base for some of their politicized assertions, to evaluate a little more objectively than has been the case to date how much and what kind of real damage was done, and perhaps formulate recommendations that could serve as guidelines to prevent recurrence of such bizarre incidents, as well as perhaps abate the sporadic guerrilla warfare between some of the more vocal but partially uninformed behavioral scientists and their Government.

Dr. Blair and Dr. Morse, with others, castigate the secular missionary disguised as social scientist, social engineer, or in numerous other masquerades of nationalistic ethnocentrism. Dr. Morse calls him an "insufferable meddler." Dr. Morse wants to stop the computer because for him it merely multiplies false cures for hysteria, as phenomena in Latin America are viewed by social scientists and engineers, to be cured by their disciplinary or supra-disciplinary hypnosis. If I understand what he says, historians have better answers. As an historian I am bound by inclination and guild-ties to agree with him. So, as often happens in history, what he thought was an unlikely event actually came to pass: someone has accepted his diagnosis.

As such things are wont to do, Dr. Morse's prescription involves the proposed restructuring of U.S. culture, and especially its system of higher education. I am as perplexed as he professes to be about the feasibility of such an operation. He takes the possibly preposterous position that students should be people, should learn about sexes, passions, poignancies, morality, ironies, faith, and should become mature. I differ from him on these matters only in that I would require a *Wanderjahr* in the area for incipient Latin Americanists, free from any academic "goals" but devoted to doing something interesting. I was fortunate enough to have had such an opportunity, and from it can testify that sinning beats reading about it, even in Dante's *Inferno*.

Like Dr. Adams, who seemingly wants governments without politicians, or Dr. Blair, who would like to have social scientists without arrogance, Dr. Morse would like to have academia without careerists. Who wouldn't? But the maladies (in Morse's view) which foment them —affluence and specialization—are again a very evident part of the real macrocosm, of which academia and the disciplines are a microcosm. Just as we accept the concept that 99 guilty should go free if one innocent escapes false imprisonment through the operation of our judicial system, so I am willing to let the present academic system operate without tinkering and spew out 99 careerists if it from time to time in some mystical, unengineered fashion occasionally can produce a learned and humane scholar. Somehow it does.

I am not at all certain that Morse's final, reluctant recommendation to establish one or two really first class institutes for the study and teaching of Latin American history is a useful answer. As a skeptical historian and pragmatic administrator I can envisage how such a place (or places) might develop much as has the Pan American Union. Into that one bureaucracy are built most of the structural defects of all the bureaucracies of the member states. All that is really needed is for historians to read more, think more, and write less but better. For some years the Hispanic Foundation has been under pressure to establish some research professors for those purposes, as well as some early post-doctoral and even pre-doctoral posts, to form as a continuing seminar what Morse calls an "asylum from the ratrace." I have on hand voluntary applications from numerous self-nominated possible professors for what would turn out to be the second or third such posts to be founded. In my own mind there is no question as to whom I would appoint as the first: me. Thus the *raza cósmica* could perpetuate itself.

Inadvertently I am sure I have fed some of the paranoia that practitioners of literary studies often display when surrounded by social scientists, and even historians, on panels such as this by deferring comments on Dr. Dauster's paper until the last, and out of alphabetical order.

Again it seems to me that Dr. Dauster has skillfully described for his field or fields of interest a segment of academia which has several serious problems. They seemingly stem from general structural short-comings in the training of American graduate students common to many disciplines other than Latin American literature. Within the memory of most of us were language requirements in history for German and French only, without substitutions of Spanish, Portuguese, or even Nahuatl, laid down by departments whose members were U.S. or European historians who often thought that anything west of the Hudson or south of Connecticut was "exotic." I am not sure how we ameliorated the situation, but I do know that it was not by confrontation politics.

As an ex-dean, I am wary of being led into the labyrinth of discussions about what a Ph.D. is or should be, and how to solve the common problems of reducing the drop-out rate or to shortening the stretch-out period. Nor am I professionally competent to evaluate either Dr. Dauster's analyses of the problems facing his particular guild, or their possible solutions. I am merely happy to learn that from 1962–64 some 53 doctorates in Latin American literature were earned.

How many are needed annually to provide adequate staffing for the national educational enterprise? Perhaps for this, as well as other specialties, we need market studies as well as quality controls. Reverting to my true colors as a scholarly bureaucrat I would ask if the present survival-of-the-fittest (or most persistent) syndrome, wasteful and brutal as it may appear, may not be nature's way of keeping the academic population in balance, given the fact we do not seem to have equivalent of The Pill for scholarly birth-control.

In glancing back over these random remarks, one final matter occurs to me. Implicitly or explicitly the previous speakers seem to agree that no one from outside should meddle with anything in Latin America, nor do more than analyze (but not change) the institutions and value systems, rooted deeply in medieval traditions. If these Latin American realities are all laudable and inviolable, by what authority do the speakers propose similar meddling in American universities, and the society and its government which supports the latter, equally rooted in medieval values? Viva non-intervention!

Research Opportunities and Problems in Latin America in 1968

CHARLES WAGLEY
The study of Latin American society and culture is today in fashion. In fact, never before has there been a time when scholarly interest in Latin America has been so intense in the United States, in Great Britain, in France, in West Germany, in Holland, and even in Japan. The Ford Foundation, to mention only one source of funds, has invested millions of dollars in developing Latin American studies in the United States and abroad. Spanish as spoken in Latin America and Portuguese of Brazil are languages considered crucial to our national interests. Thus, the study of these languages and the study of the societies of Latin America warrant graduate fellowships from the Federal Government, which also supports directly a series of Language and Area Centers in our universities. Each year sees the creation of one or more new Latin American research and teaching centers or institutes at universities in the United States and in Europe. This, in brief, is the general climate or atmosphere within which we must dis-

cuss research opportunities and problems in Latin America. It must be stated at once, however, that the present state of dynamic growth and of affluence may hardly endure in view of the modified policies of several foundations and the inability of the Federal Government to expand its support.

The renewed interest in Latin America during the last decade, sparked by ample financing from several sources, has produced a flood of new research in all fields of the social sciences and the humanities. As perhaps a necessary side effect, it has also produced numerous surveys of research under way and of the status of our present knowledge in different disciplines. The Joint Committee of Latin American Studies (SSRC-ACLS) has published two volumes, *Social Science Research on Latin America* and *Social Science Research in Latin America*,[1] which give broad coverage to the status of research and point out specific areas in which research is needed. The newly founded Latin American Studies Association publishes three times a year the *Latin American Research Review,* in which excellent review articles have appeared on recent research and on further research needs; and this review carries news items of research in progress by scholars in the United States and abroad. The journal, *Aportes,* published in France and the *Boletín Informativo* . . . issued by Center of Study and Documentation for Latin America in Amsterdam tell us of the work being done by Europeans on Latin America. And, from Latin America, such journals as *América Latina* and *Revista Latino-americana de Sociología* bring news of publications and research in progress. These are but a few of the many research aids and research reviews which the new era of affluence in Latin American studies has brought to us.

When I look at the large mass of research under way and the large number of books and articles on Latin America that appear each month, I wonder why I ever accepted the invitation to speak on the subject of research opportunities and problems—and I find that I cannot discuss this broad subject without added reflection upon the climate for research in Latin America.

The affluence of Latin American studies in the last decade has brought mixed blessings. On the positive side, a large number of first-rate graduate students have been attracted into Latin American studies when in the past they might well have specialized in Europe, Asia, Africa, or Russian studies. Many of them come to graduate school already fluent in either Spanish or Portuguese and many with experience in Latin America provided by one of the many undergraduate field programs. There have been programs to retrain in Latin American studies young Ph.D.s whose graduate degrees were in another area. Furthermore, established scholars well known for their work in their own disciplines have been drawn into Latin American research and have brought fresh insights and theoretical awareness. "Old Latin American hands," such as myself, have funds for research and a broader and more interested audience for what they write. The last decade has changed the face of Latin American studies and research; it will always be richer and more interesting than it was before.

But, as indicated above, I have apprehensions about the affluence and the sudden spurt of interest in Latin American studies. Some of my apprehensions are not unique at all to Latin America but concern also other areas of the world. First, it is obvious to all of us that almost every country in Latin America is flooded with researchers from the United States. Chiapas and Oaxaca, for example, are over-populated with anthropologists; most of the few remaining tribal groups of Amazonia have resident ethnologists. The archives and libraries of Latin America are flooded by U.S. historians. Political scientists interview over and over again the same political leaders. In Rio de Janeiro, in 1964, almost thirty Ph.D. candidates were at work collecting data for their dissertations.[2] One director of a Latin American research and teaching institution complained bitterly that he had neither the time, staff, facilities, nor funds to take care of or even be civil to the constant stream of pre- and post-doctoral researchers that sought help from his organization. Added to the burden of numerous United States researchers is the fact that Latin American officials and scholars are understandably nervous about so many foreign social scientists inquiring into their society and documents. After the publicity given to Project Camelot and to the penetration of CIA into research and academic organizations, cooperation with U.S. social scientists may even bring adverse local criticism to a Latin American institution or to his Latin American colleagues. Thus, affluence, plus government activities beyond our control, has resulted in closing off some areas of social science research and making research in general more difficult than it was before.

Second, the affluence of Latin American studies often leads to research with a grand design—the study of social mobility in five nations, the attitudes of university students in three countries, the study of land tenure systems across the board. There is no intention to demean large comparative programs, for such research is much needed, and it is often well planned and well executed. But it is the consequences in terms of research personnel that give me pause. They offer opportunity to North American graduate students and they occupy the relatively few well trained Latin American social scientists usefully and lucratively. But, they often divert these same North American graduate students and Latin Americans from their training and teaching functions and sometimes, I am told, from their own individual research.

Third, our affluence (and that of Europe) in Latin American studies has caused a "brain drain" in Latin American social science. It is not only those Latin Americans who have left their countries to take positions in the United States, in Europe, or with international organizations that I refer to. One must recognize the poverty of the academic career in most of Latin America and the frequent lack of liberty of action in some countries which drives Latin Americans abroad. But, it is also a fact that a relatively small circle of Latin American social scientists, mainly individuals who were trained abroad or in their own countries in more parsimonious days, have joined the "jet set." The same names with little variation are seen on the programs of conferences in New York, London, Paris, Münster, Santiago de Chile, and elsewhere and the same people appear as visiting professors and lecturers in various United States universities and in Europe. One wonders how they can do their own research and if they are training a new generation of Latin American students to take their places. It is true that there are excellent research and training institutions such as FLACSO in Chile, the Di Tella Institute in Argentina, El Colegio de México, the new graduate school of Political Science in Minas Gerais (Brazil) and others where Latin American students are being trained and are doing important research. But, unless a very much larger number of highly qualified Latin American social scientists are produced (and their careers made more attractive), the quasi-monopoly of social science research by foreign scholars, mainly from the U.S., will increase. This will not at all improve the climate for research by outsiders; in fact, it looks like cultural imperialism to many Latin Americans.

Unless the climate for social science improves there may not be many research opportunities for scholars from the United States in the foreseeable future. Crucial to our future research is the multiplication of Latin American social scientists, the improvement of social science in Latin America as a career, and the support of research conceived by Latin Americans, carried out by Latin Americans, and reported by Latin Americans. None of us wants to halt or reduce our own research nor to prevent our students from researching in Latin America; but the minimum that we can all do is to build into our research the training of Latin American students and the full participation of our Latin American colleagues.

The proliferation of social science research on Latin America in the last few years and the increasingly unfavorable climate for research does not mean that Latin America offers any less of an open, free, and rich field for such research. Most Latin American colleagues welcome the individual scholar and the Latin American general public has infinite patience with our questions and questionnaires. There is an infinite range of research to be done in all disciplines. But the growing body of data and the growing sophistication of Latin American specialists in all disciplines mean that research today must be more sharply focused and more specific than ever before. The time has passed when books or articles which aim to treat Latin America as a whole—even when limited to a single institution or a problem such as the Church, the military, or the problem of occupation and social stratification—make any fundamental contribution. Such papers can be stimulating when they are symposia which distill the work of a group of authors on a single subject. Today, a research report that genuinely contributes to the accumulated knowledge of Latin America must treat a specific subject in a limited time and place. This does not mean that a research project should not be comparative; in fact, Latin America lends itself to the comparative method—when variables are controlled and the subject limited. In sum, this seems to be a time for highly specialized research on Latin America. There are too many theories about Latin America based upon the same monographs and the same old data. We need some new monographs with new data for new theories. And it is the individual scholar with a limited research program who has the best chance of contributing today to Latin American study.

With this background, I should like to turn more specifically to research problems and opportunities in Latin America. I feel that I must do so within my own field of specialization, namely social anthropology, and in related disciplines. To advise others on their own disciplines at this stage in the development of Latin American studies would be presumptuous to say the least. When I seek to advise others regarding new research problems and opportunities in social or cultural anthropology, I ask myself several types of questions. What are the pieces of research already reported in the literature which have taught me most about Latin America or any part of it? What research carried out in Latin America has contributed most to the general theory and substance of social anthropology? What research in Latin America in closely related disciplines has contributed most to my understanding of anthropological data and to my understanding of theory? What methods, what theories, and what problems have been studied in other world areas that might be applied to Latin America? What problems unique to Latin America seem to have been neglected? Research in Latin America is like research elsewhere in the world—it should be conceived in terms of one's discipline and within a broad comparative perspective.

Some of the research projects in my own discipline which have taught me most about Latin America were group undertakings. They were carried out by teams of anthropologists led by a senior scholar. Two examples of such research projects were the studies under the direction of Robert Redfield in Yucatán in the 1930s[3] and that carried out by Julian Steward and his associates in Puerto Rico in 1948–50. Both of these projects involved field research by different individuals following a preconceived plan in several localities. Both of them resulted in a body of substantive data about Yucatán and Puerto Rican communities and a set of hypotheses and conclusions that have influenced profoundly the methodology, the research, and the theory of social anthropologists. In each of these projects, it was not only the theoretical and synthetic contributions of the senior scholars but the individual contributions of the individual researchers, such as Alfonso Villa Rojas, Sidney Mintz, Eric Wolf, Robert Manners, and others which were important.

Certainly, the team approach and the constant interaction between the individual researchers seem to have been mutually stimulating and highly productive. With the increase of funds for research, roughly similar team studies in social anthropology continue to be an important mechanism by which social anthropological research is done in Latin America. One only needs to cite the team research by Ralph Beals and associates in Oaxaca (Mexico), the long-term research by Evon Vogt and associates among the Maya-speaking Indians of Chiapas (Mexico) and the studies being carried out in six communities in Bolivia for the Peace Corps by Lambros Comitas and associates. Most of these team projects, even today, are carried through without serious incident and they often contribute to the development of social anthropology locally by training and using Latin American assistants. But, they also contribute, in a highly visible form, to the flood of foreign researchers into limited regions of Latin America. With the growing climate of irritation, suspicion, and even antagonism toward North American researchers, the time for such team endeavors may be running out. At least, some of them are bound to aggravate an increasingly tense situation.

It would seem to me that the research climate today calls for individual research. When I look back over the great contributions to Latin American research in social anthropology, I find that much of it has been by individuals. I think at once, for example, of the work of Kurt Nimendaju, a German ethnologist resident of Brazil, who between 1920 and 1945 carried out a large series of studies among the tribal groups of central Brazil.[4] His research completely modified the picture of aboriginal ethnography of the lowland tribes, and his work is even now being extended and corrected by contemporary social anthropologists such as William Crocker, David Maybury-Lewis, Roberto Cardoso de Oliveira, and others. There are still lowland tribes of South America which have never been studied (and some are as yet unpacified); I refer especially to those in the region of the northern headwaters of the Amazon between Brazil, Colombia, Venezuela, and the Guianas. And, even more important for research on highly focused problems of human ecology, on small group behavior, on social tensions and the like, there are the many tribal groups already in contact with the Western world and for which the basic ethnographic surveys have already been done such as the Bororo, Tapirape, Caraja, and others. The day of aboriginal ethnography is not yet over in Latin America. By necessity, aboriginal ethnology is individual research or collaborative endeavor of no more than two people.

As I look back over the research history of my discipline in Latin America, it seems to me that Melville Herskovits left a rich heritage—

and one that has been neglected by recent research. His lifetime work on the Negro in the New World, which carried him to Haiti,[5] Surinam,[6] Trinidad,[7] Brazil,[8] and even to Africa itself,[9] was continued by many of his students and younger men such as Rene Ribeiro, Villiam Bascom, Rui Coelho, Octavio Costa Eduardo, Ruth Landes and others. Herskovits left us numerous research hypotheses,[10] only one of which has been properly developed and used; namely, that the matrifocal family was an African survival in the New World which set off a long series of studies and debates on the family in the Caribbean. In recent years, the study of African cultures in the New World has been neglected by American social anthropologists at a time when a comparative view of the adaptation of the African to the national societies of America has become so important. In Arnold Strickon's review of the state of anthropological research in *Social Science Research on Latin America,* the subject of research on the African in the New World is mentioned only in passing and the name of Melville Herskovits does not even figure in the bibilography.[11]

Our present knowledge of the traditional Afro-American fetish cults such as the *candomble* of Brazil and Haitian *Vodun* is limited mainly to religious ideology and the ritual.[12] One wonders how these cults are integrated into modern urban society? What role do these cults play in the lives of people who work in factories and in large bureaucratic structures? What is the budget of a traditional Bahian *candomble* which owns property and puts on elaborate feasts? But, even more important than the traditional cults seem to be new and less traditional religious sects which have taken root in the great cities of South Brazil and claim literally hundreds of thousands of members. The Umbanda movement of Brazil, for example, seems to be a syncretism of African, Spiritist, and traditional Christian belief and ritual, and it is organized into various federations of individual cults or *terreiros* which exert political and economic power over their members. Surely, these new religions offer the social anthropologist a new field for research.

Studies of the aboriginal cultures and of the African in the New World immediately brings to mind the field of ethnohistory. In the past, anthropologists generally had to do their own ethnohistory and even today it is a field of research that almost by necessity combines social anthropology, sociology, and history. Elman Service[13] and Louis Faron,[14] both social anthropologists, provided us with lucid studies of the *encomienda* system as it functioned in Paraguay and in Chile as a background, so to speak, for their ethnological research. Florestan Fernandes, sociologist who is best known for his studies of contemporary Brazil, first appeared in print as an ethnohistorian. His two books on the social organization and on the function of warfare among the extinct Tupinambá Indians of the Brazilian coast are models of the application of sociological and anthropological theory to historical data.[15] And yet, ethnohistory has been, and is being done, by historians. One should never forget the well-known studies by Woodrow Borah, Sherburne Cooke, and Lesley Simpson on the population of Mexico which has entirely modified the view of anthropologists of the aboriginal civilizations. And, above all, one must cite the ethnohistorical work of Charles Gibson in Mexico, which has culminated in his magnificent book *The Aztecs under Spanish Rule.*[16] Similarly, no one can understand the present problems of the Indian and the peasant in Mexico without reading *Métodos y resultados de la política indigenista de México* which was written by a group of anthropologists and historians.[17]

Ethnohistory is a very rich field of research for sociologists, anthropologists, and historians, particularly in Latin America. Perhaps for no other area of the world do we have such rich data on the fusion of peoples of diverse origins as in Latin America. In 1940, this field of research was certainly marginal to various disciplines; today it is a recognized and active field of research. In the 1965 edition of the *Handbook of Latin American Studies,* there is a separate section devoted to publications (187 in number) on ethnohistory in Mesoamerica[18] and a journal devoted to ethnohistory publishes articles on Latin America and other areas.

Closely related to ethnohistory is the study of the history of slavery as an institution, the slave trade, the African origins of the Negroes who were brought to the New World, and race relations as it changed over time in the Americas. Magnus Mörner has provided us with an excellent review of the status of research in some of these fields of interest;[19] it is evident from his survey that the study of such problems has hardly begun. As in ethnohistory this is a field of tremendous interest to the social anthropologist and the sociologist, and the historian who undertakes such studies must be well versed in sociology and anthropology. The work of Sidney Mintz (an anthropologist) on Caribbean social history; of Octavio Ianni and Fernando Henrique Cardoso (both sociologists) on slavery in Southern Brazil, and of

Magnus Mörner (a historian) on race relations immediately come to mind.

And, above all, when I think of the contribution of social anthropology to Latin American studies, I think of the numerous community studies ranging from Redfield's early study of Tepoztlán in 1928 to that by N. E. Whitten of a coastal Ecuadorian community in 1963.[20] In other places, I have several times before pointed to the need for additional community studies in certain geographical areas and for studies of a variety of community types.[21] Still, to my knowledge there are no full fledged community studies of any kind for Chile, Venezuela, Honduras, Nicaragua, Panama, the Dominican Republic, Cuba, or Southern Brazil. Arnold Strickon's unpublished study of an Argentine ranching community is still the only community study for that nation that I am aware of. Furthermore, most Latin American community studies are predominantly of small peasant communities; more studies of plantation and hacienda communities, of larger market towns, and even of small cities are needed.

Yet, I would not urge the proliferation of community studies simply to fill in the regional and community-type lacunae—as useful as most community studies have proven to be for the understanding of Latin American society. I do hope, however, that my colleagues will continue to do research in communities. The local community, and especially those which have already been studied, offer an excellent locus-laboratory for research on problems such as race relations, the socialization of the child, the structure of the family, the effectiveness of directed or planned programs of development, the power structure or another specific problem or a limited aspect of the community society or culture.

Then, the traditional field techniques of community study seem to lend themselves to research on other groups or sub-units of a large community. In recent years, social anthropologists and others have carried out considerable work on urban shanty towns or squatter settlements within large cities. Although much of the ethnographic detail still remains to be published, William Mangin[22] has given us a very useful survey of the research done and some of the problems as yet to be studied in such urban settlements. And, Mangin has also studied urban voluntary associations composed of migrants from specific rural regions of Peru using research methods similar to those used in studying a community.

Two research projects as yet incomplete which are being carried out for doctoral dissertations in anthropology at Columbia University fall into this category. They strike me as especially worth mentioning because they use community study methods on social units other than the small community. One of them has been referred to above, namely the Umbanda religious movement in Brazil being studied by Diana Brown. As stated earlier, this movement has several federations or associations of Umbanda sects, with officers and rules and regulations governing the various local "churches" or "terreiros." The individual churches are scattered about the large cities of Brazil, especially in Rio de Janeiro and in São Paulo. Most of them are composed of the urban lower class but many are made up of people of the middle class. Certainly considerable quantitative data must be gathered (or is available in Umbanda federation headquarters) regarding the social and economic situation of the total membership,[23] but selected individual churches may easily be studied using the techniques of participant observation and multiple interviews of the type used traditionally by anthropologists. The results of such research promises to furnish not only insight into the religious ideology of the cult members but considerable information on the attitudes, values, and aspirations of the lower middle class in the urban environment.

The second research project, which is now being completed by Charles Wilson, is the study of four factories in Mexico City. Three of these factories were small enough to be studied as small groups (i.e. between 50 and 150 workers) while a department or a sub-division of the larger factory provided comparable data. Again, considerable quantitative data had to be gathered on industrial organizations in Mexico City in order to place the factories studied within local perspective. The research was done by participant-observation and by interviews. The entire personnel—from the ownership-management to the workers of these factories—were viewed as a social system and an attempt was made to follow the factory personnel into their home environments. Mr. Wilson's analysis of his data showed the extraordinary importance of kinship, *compadrazgo,* and personalism—all highly traditional Latin American traits—in the relationships among the factory workers and between the workers and the administration. Again, one of the side benefits of his study is considerable substantive data and objective insight into the total culture of factory workers in Mexico City. Both studies illustrate well the opportunity for seeking new types of social units for research analysis. There is no reason why mental hospitals which have been studied in the United States cannot be studied in Latin America. And there are numerous other organizations and social groups—labor unions, social clubs, religious brotherhoods, and the like that would lend themselves to this type of research.

In addition, social anthropologists have become interested in recent years in the relationship of individual communities within a large societal system. Particularly in India, "networks" of communication and interaction based upon marriage, kinship, caste, markets, and religious pilgrimages which interconnect and interrelate villages over a wide region have been studied.[24] In Norway, John Barnes writes about "country-wide networks" of kinsmen, friends, associations and groups which interconnect across boundaries of community and social class.[25] For Latin America specifically, Eric Wolf theorized on the importance of a type of individual whom he called a "culture broker," who was able to act both in terms of the local community and in terms of the larger society, and who served as intermediary between the local community and the larger society.[26] And, Frank Young and his associates at Cornell University have proposed a system of identifying and analyzing networks of communities based upon interviews with "key informants" on the presence and absence of community and inter-community institutions and services.[27]

But, the research on inter-community networks still needs to be done in Latin America, although I understand that Young's system of analysis has been essayed in Puerto Rico and Guatemala. To my knowledge, no one has actually undertaken research on the "culture broker" in a specific community in Latin America, although such people are easy to identify and all of us agree upon their importance. Sidney Mintz in the West Indies and Ralph Beals in Oaxaca in Mexico have been studying markets, which are certainly an important key to inter-community relations. And Fernando Cámara in Mexico has begun a project to study religious pilgrimages and religious brotherhoods which seem to form networks of related villages and communities to a central religious shrine. Other possibilities of inter-community research might involve studies of the function of kinship among the local and regional elite,[28] or it might involve studies of the power structure both within communities and within sets or networks of local communities using techniques similar to those of Floyd Hunter's reputational method.[29] Research on inter-community networks, regional ties, and other supra-community phenomena by anthropologists in Latin America is just beginning. This kind of research seems to me to be of especial importance for I am more and more convinced that the local community alone is seldom the strategic or feasible unit for development.

From my discussion and the examples cited above of the research I would like to see done in social anthropology, it should not be difficult to ferret out what kind of research I would like to see done in disciplines other than my own. I find that I learn most from what might be called monographs—from detailed studies of a circumscribed unit in a limited time and place. Such monographs must be placed in a broad perspective which gives them more than unique significance. Stanley Stein's study of Vassouras[30] limited mainly to one *municipio* between 1850 and 1900 but interpreted in broad terms provided me with more fresh insights into Brazilian history than did the erudite and very general economic histories of Brazil by Caio Prado Júnior.[31]

Just as the local community has provided a focus of research for the social anthropologist, it is to be hoped that the sociologist, the political scientist, the social psychologist, and even the economist will focus their unit of research and provide us with rich data in monographs— or, if you like, broadly conceived case studies. If the sociologist wants to study university students, I wish that he would do research on the students at the University of Bahia or the University of Guadalajara— or at most a comparative study of two provincial and traditionally minded universities. From political scientists, I would like to have concrete monographic studies of political institutions and political behavior as they exist within the framework of villages, towns, municipalities, and cities. From geographers, I feel the need of more ecological studies of human adaptation in limited areas such as Parsons' study of the Antioqueño central highlands of Colombia or even of more limited areas such as Sternberg's study of the community of Careiro,[32] near Manaus in the Brazilian Amazon. Obviously, economists must draw their statistical data from a regional or a national context but even in economics a monographic or case study approach seems to pay off. Hirschman's insightful *Journeys Toward Progress* was based upon a rather thorough analysis of three case studies—planning in Northeastern Brazil, land reform programs in Colombia, and the problem of containing inflation in Chile.[33]

The climate for research in Latin America today favors my inclinations. It seems to me to be a time for the individual researcher. I have heard it said that the day of the individual research scholar is over and that social science research must be by teams drawn from various disciplines. I am not persuaded that this is so. Even more, I feel sure that it is not so for Latin America.[34] One of the encouraging aspects of doing research in the Latin American field is that the individual doctoral dissertation can be a real contribution to knowledge.

Finally, the point of view which I have taken vis-à-vis research seems to me to have some implications regarding training and the organization of curricula in our universities. The individual researcher must be highly prepared in his own discipline but be able to interpret his research in broad terms. This does not mean that he must be any more interdisciplinary than a researcher who works in other parts of the world. Latin America is not a particularly exotic world area. The major languages are familiar European tongues "with a difference" and the major institutions are recognizably European. Today all research scholars must be interdisciplinary in many ways. If you are a social anthropologist doing research in the United States, you must speak English; you must know something of United States history, you must be acquainted with sociological and political studies that have been done in the United States; and you must have read something of its literature. One would expect the same range of knowledge of anyone doing research in France, Germany, or one of the Latin American countries. The new generation entering Latin American research knows Spanish and Portuguese (and sometimes a smattering of Nahuatl or Quechua). They read the novels for fun and for insights. They take courses in history, not just to get a degree or certificate, but to help them understand the society and the culture in which they hope to do research. But, they also know that they must be well trained anthropologists, historians, sociologists, or political scientists. They must be, above all, modern, creative scholars in their own discipline. The day of "area specialists" or "Latin Americanists" is over.

NOTES   1. Charles Wagley, ed., *Social Science Research on Latin America* (New York: Columbia University Press, 1964); Manuel Diégues Júnior and Bryce Wood, eds., *Social Science Research in Latin America* (New York: Columbia University Press, 1967).

2. Robert Levine, ed., *Brazil: A Field Research Guide in the Social Sciences* (New York: Institute of Latin American Studies, Columbia University, 1966).

3. Robert Redfield, *The Folk Culture of Yucatan* (Chicago: University of Chicago Press, 1941).

4. Kurt Nimendaju, *The Apinaje* (Berkeley: University of California Press, 1939); *The Sherente* (Los Angeles: Publications of the Friedrich Webb Hodge Anniversary Fund, 1942); *The Eastern Timbira* (Berkeley: University of California Press, 1946).

5. Melville Herskovits, *Life in a Haitian Valley* (New York: A. A. Knopf, 1937).

6. Melville and Francis F. Herskovits, *Rebel Destiny: Among the Bush Negroes of Dutch Guiana* (New York: McGraw-Hill, 1934); and *Suriname Folklore* (New York: Columbia University Press, 1936).

7. Melville and Francis F. Herskovits, *Trinidad Village* (New York: A. A. Knopf, 1947).

8. Melville Herskovits, "The Negro in Bahia, Brazil: A Problem of Method," *American Sociological Review*, VIII: 4 (August 1943): 394–404.

9. Melville Herskovits, *The Myth of the Negro Past* (New York: Harper & Brothers, 1941); and *Dahomey*, 2 (New York: J. J. Agustin, 1938).

10. Herskovits, *The Myth, op. cit.*

11. Arnold Strickon, "Anthology in Latin America," in *Social Science Research on Latin America*, ed., Charles Wagley, *op. cit.*, pp. 125–165.

12. George E. Simpson, "The Belief of Haitian Vodun," *American Anthropologist*, XLVII: 1 (January–March 1946): 35–59; "The Sango Cult in Nigeria and Trinidad," *American Anthropologist*, XLIV: 6 (December 1962): 1204–1219.

13. Elman Service, "Spanish-Guaraní Relations in Early Colonial Paraguay," *Anthropological Papers*, University of Michigan, 1954, no. 9.

14. Louis C. Faron, "Effects of Conquest on the Araucanian Picunche during the Spanish Colonization of Chile: 1536–1635," *Ethnohistory*, VII (1960): 239–307.

15. Florestan Fernandes, *A organização social dos Tupinambá* (São Paulo: Instituto Progreso Editorial, 1949); *A função social da guerra na sociedade Tupinambá* (São Paulo, 1952).

16. Charles Gibson, *The Aztecs under Spanish Rule: A History of the Indians of the Valley of México: 1510–1810*, (Palo Alto, California: Stanford University Press, 1964).

17. Alfonso Caso y otros, "Métodos y resultados de la política indigenista en México," *Memorias del Instituto Nacional Indigenista*, VI (México, 1954).

18. Harold B. Nicholson, "Ethnohistory," in *Handbook of Latin American Studies* no. 27 (Gainesville, Florida: University of Florida Press, 1965), pp. 75–96. Peruvian ethnohistory has been researched by John H. Rowe, "Inca Culture at the Time of the Spanish Conquest," *Handbook of South American Indians*, ed., S. J. Haynes (New York: Cooper Square Publishers, 1946), II, pp. 183–330; John Murra, "Social Structure and Economic Themes in Andean Ethnohistory," *Anthropological Quarterly*, XXXIV: 2 (April 1961): 47–59; and George Kluber, *The Indian Caste of Peru, 1795–1940* (Washington, D.C.: Government Printing Office, 1952); and "The

Quechua and the Colonial World," in *Handbook of South American Indians, op. cit.,* pp. 331–410.

19. Magnus Mörner, "The History of Race Relations in Latin America: Some Comments on the State of Research," *Latin American Research Review,* I: 3 (Summer 1967): 65–98.

20. Robert Redfield, *Tepoztlán, A Mexican Village* (Chicago: University of Chicago Press, 1930); Norman E. Whitten, *Class, Kinship and Power in an Ecuadorian Town* (Palo Alto, California: Stanford University Press, 1965).

21. Charles Wagley and Marvin Harris, "A Typology of Latin American Subcultures," *American Anthropologist,* LVII: 3 (June 1955): 428–451; Charles Wagley, *The Latin American Tradition* (New York: Columbia University Press, 1968).

22. William Mangin, "Latin American Squatter Settlements: A Problem and a Solution," *Latin American Research Review,* II: 3 (Summer 1967): 65–98.

23. 28,000 "churches" or *terreiros* were listed by one federation in the states of Guanabara and Rio de Janeiro in 1965. See Diana Brown, "The Practice of Umbanda in Rio de Janeiro," a field report, 26 pages (mimeographed).

24. McKim Mariott and Bernard Cohn, "Networks and Centers in the Integration of Indian Civilization," *Journal of Social Research* (Bihar, India), 1958, I. Robert Redfield, "Civilizations as Societal Structures: The Development of Community Structures," in *Human Nature and Study of Society* (Chicago, 1962), pp. 375–391.

25. John Barnes, "Class and Committees in a Norwegian Island Parish," *Human Relations,* VII (1954): 39–58.

26. Eric Wolf, "Aspects of Group Relations in a Complex Society: México," *American Anthropologist,* LVIII: 6 (December 1956): 1065–1078.

27. Frank W. Young, "A Proposal for Cooperative Cross-Cultural Research on Inter-Village Systems," *Human Organization,* XXV: 1 (Spring 1966): 46–50.

28. Arnold Strickon, "Class and Kinship in Argentina," *Ethnology,* I: 4 (October 1962): 500–515.

29. William D'Antonio and William Form, *Influentials in Two Border Cities: A Study in Community Decision Making* (Milwaukee, Wisconsin: University of Notre Dame Press, 1965); Harold R. Edward, "Power Structure and its Communication Behavior in San José, Costa Rica," *Journal of Inter-American Studies,* IX: 2 (April 1967): 236–245.

30. Stanley J. Stein, *Vassouras: A Brazilian Coffee Country, 1850–1900,* (Cambridge, Massachusetts: Harvard University Press, 1957).

31. Caio Prado Júnior, *Formação do Brasil contemporâneo* (São Paulo, 1942), *Historia econômica do Brasil* (São Paulo, 1945).

32. James Parsons, "Antioqueño Colonization in Western Colombia," *Ibero-Americana,* XXXII (1949); Hilgard O'Reilly Sternberg, *A agua e o homen na várzea do Careiro* (Rio de Janeiro, 1956).

33. Albert O. Hirschman, *Journeys Toward Progress: Studies of Economic Policy-Making in Latin America* (New York: Twentieth Century Fund, 1963).

34. In the history of Latin American research, there have been team endeavours with a grand design that have been successful. The long-term study of Mexican modern history led by Daniel Cosío Villegas (see Stanley R. Ross, "Cosío Villegas, Historia Moderna de México," *Hispanic American Historical Review*, XLVI: 3 (August 1966): 274–282, seems to me one of them; but evidently Cosío Villegas treated each collaborator as an individual scholar, and all of them were historians.

Commentary*

ANTONIO ALATORRE   I am afraid something will backfire in these commentaries of mine. Dr. Wagley is an eminent North American social anthropologist. I am not eminent, not a social anthropologist, nor am I North American. We have only one thing in common: we have dedicated our lives to study and research. It is clear that the commentaries of other eminent Latin Americanists, who speak from the North American viewpoint, will have to be more relevant and more orthodox than mine. However, I have much confidence that our status as scholars is a unifying factor and is surely much more important than those which separate us. Dr. Wagley's paper is so solid, so full of data and first-hand information, and it is so honest and sincere, there is difficulty in finding subject-matter for discussion. Especially when he, himself, with exemplary self-criticism, anticipates any possible objections.

First, there are some of the problems that refer to the presence

* Translation by Mauricio Charpenel.

of the North American researcher in Latin American countries. Dr. Wagley speaks of an exhaustion of patience among us and seems to say that we are already tired of a kind of North American invasion or saturation. This is true in many cases, but not always. Tiredness or impatience depend on many factors. Above all, on the nature of the research, on the orientation or work method and, naturally, on the preparation and intelligence of the North American researcher who is visiting us.

I will illustrate this with a personal case. Certainly I am annoyed by the post-graduate student who comes to see me at El Colegio de México, with a questionnaire mimeographed here in his university, concerning given uses of spoken Spanish in Mexico in order to elaborate from it his doctoral dissertation. I have had two incidents of this nature lately. The students did not seem to me to be brilliant; I found them to be not well-oriented and, above all, their methodology of using a questionnaire fabricated prior to their contact with the language of Mexico seems to me erroneous. It is obvious that my collaboration with them has not been wholehearted. Is it worthwhile to give time to research that is not going to produce good results?

In reality, one of these inquiries, one of these questionnaires, was worse than the other because it came by mail. The interested party did not show up. At the conclusion of the questionnaire, I was asked to furnish five names and addresses of persons skilled in the Spanish language in Mexico and I, lying impudently, told him that I was the only one who could answer this.

Some colleagues from El Colegio de México, in the fields of history, economics and political sciences have spoken to me of analogous experiences, but I must add immediately that these cases are not that frequent and my colleagues from the Colegio agree on this. In reality, the North American researcher who visits us is generally well prepared, and it is needless to say that in that case there is no weariness or impatience but only the desire to aid good research.

And here we approach another subject, the advantages of the North American researcher over the Latin American. Far be it for me to think that the North American is more intelligent and far be it, too, for me to cast any shadow of resentful nationalism over this discussion. What I will do is to comment upon a fact.

Dr. Wagley has spoken to us of the progress of social anthropology in Latin America and of the role that the North American researchers have had in its flourishing. In my field of literature and linguistics, the role of North American Latin Americanists has perhaps not been as spectacular, but it would be easy to enumerate examples of brilliant research in linguistics and, above all, in literature whose completion was possible partially because the researcher was North American. North American students are much better prepared than are our students. Their libraries are well supplied; their archives are marvelously organized. In one word, they have confidence in an intellectual world that functions; from the start they have a feeling of security that is not frequently found in our students, deprived almost always during their formative years of all those facilities that not only act on the development of intelligence but also on the affirmation of the person.

The prototype of the North American researcher is for me the young professor who goes to Mexico to study the poet López Velarde, who has read previously, in his university, all his works and all that has been written about him, and has become perfectly well-acquainted with post-modernist literature, and who in Mexico travels from one place to another, goes not only to the capital, but also to Guadalajara, to San Luis Potosí, Aguascalientes and Zacatecas, speaks with the descendants of the poet and with the persons who knew him, examines family archives, takes photocopies of letters, literary manuscripts, and forgotten printed matter and, during this period of time, has lived with us and becomes one of us; he has a great time and then to top it off writes directly in Spanish his renovating book on the poet.

At times it is not the training of the North American which is in question. A colleague from El Colegio de México told me about a recent case. It concerned a young United States researcher who went to Mexico to study how the PRI works. The PRI, as you know, is the only political party that counts in Mexico. He wanted to see it function not at the metaphysical level of organization and political speculation, but at a concrete and picturesque level of reality at the time of elections. It was thus necessary to interview delegates of the small villages, municipal presidents, subordinates to municipal presidents, etc. Well, these commissaries, who had not wished to be questioned by Mexican researchers, on this occasion appeared very communicative. When facing a Mexican researcher they are suspicious, they fear a trap. When facing the North American, they evidently feel safer. Without a doubt, this consideration should be added to the reasons for the success of a researcher like Oscar Lewis.

Dr. Wagley is very right when he speaks of the need to better the intellectual climate of Latin America. He talks of "the climate for Social Sciences" which I broaden slightly. He is also right in this same sense when he deplores the "brain drain" or emigration of intellectuals to the United States. Here I almost feel personally alluded to as I have just accepted an appointment that will require my coming to Princeton for a semester each year. I must say that this "brain drain" has very complex causes. The financial inducement is important and even more important is the opportunity to work in a good library.

But that is not all. It is natural that a Celso Furtado, accused of being a Communist in Brazil, looks for refuge here. That is to say not only in an excellent university medium but also in a much more politically mature country than his own, and I can add that I too have been accused in Mexico (where the intellectual environment is more propitious) of being a Communist. It is true that the accusation appeared in one of the most reactionary newspapers in Mexico, but also it is true that we don't know what is coming next.

Thus, to speak as Dr. Wagley does of the necessity of bettering the intellectual level of Latin America suggests many things. It is natural for the North American researcher to think that with improvement, his own opportunities for research will increase. The Latin American researcher necessarily has to see this problem in a more ample perspective. A new Alliance for Progress would be needed; I mean to say another Alliance of a new type, without political overtones that would cause it to flounder, in order to gain a climate of liberty without which research suffers from obstructions or becomes impossible.

If the problems were understood from a point of view of all researchers, including Latin Americans, all uncomfortable resonance to our ears would be avoided. It is not agreeable to hear that one of our countries is considered a "land of conquest" or "field of action" for the missionary spirit that is going to win for the true faith a group of savages or, worst yet, as spoils for imperialist North American expansion. If, on the other hand, we place stress on the research problems and on the liberty we all need equally, then our own ideals would be quickly encompassed within them. The missionary spirit would then refer to our own research tasks, and we would then take as land of conquest our own land. In other words, it would not be a matter of the North American researcher taking over for himself the terrain but rather that all researchers would benefit without limit from the possibility and the liberty of undertaking his task.

I proceed quickly and come to other aspects of Dr. Wagley's talk. Speaking from his specialization, social anthropology, Dr. Wagley says that in previous years the best research was that of working teams and that in the future the hour will come for the individual researcher. I do not know to what degree this understanding and this foresight can be generalized for the future. My own experience as researcher and as director of one of the centers of study of El Colegio de México, differs and here also I can mention the experience of other colleagues of mine from the Colegio. I could well say the opposite. One research project we have undertaken at the Colegio concerns Mexican Popular Lyrics, a field that in the past belonged almost exclusively to the individual researcher and that now, however, seems eminently adequate for team research. Although we must add that strictly literary research has been and will continue to be the field of the individual scholar.

In the same manner linguistic research at the Colegio on the Spanish that is spoken in Mexico is and will be conducted more and more through team work. Our experience and that of another of the study-centers of El Colegio plus that derived from the exemplary German-Mexican research project known as "Project Pueblo Atlaxcala" would point, in fact, towards an intermediate solution between team work and individual work. Dr. Wagley knows the results of one of these mixed enterprises: the Modern History of Mexico, done by a group of mature researchers under the direction of Daniel Cosío Villegas. I do not think one can generalize. The history of research will show always, I am sure, a continuous coming and going between detailed monograph and big synthesis work, but this coming and going may be, and in fact is at times, simultaneous. Even in the improbable case that an era of general synthesis is followed by monographic research the different eras certainly do not have to coincide with the different disciplines.

One last word. I said at first that it was difficult to remark on Dr. Wagley's paper. In effect, it is difficult and the reason is clear; if where he says *North American researcher,* I read only *researcher,* or where he says *social anthropology research* I read only *research,* or where he enumerates work done and important tasks to be undertaken in the future, I place other titles and other names, then what he says I can say. I too believe in the importance of specialized, well-rounded monographs although perhaps I would stress what should be understood by specialization. A specialized study on a great novel, by one author, is certainly not the same as a specialized study on a novel lacking transcendency.

I also expect a great deal. I expect light to be shed from the worthwhile research coming out of the group of our field of study. I also see that the Latin American area offers an elective field for comparative studies, but there is no need to continue this enumeration. The important thing is that the faith and the optimism of Dr. Wagley is shared by me and by many university people from Latin America. That is to say that even if there are secondary differences we speak, in fact, the same language and we think the same things. And it is certainly comforting not only to know but to confirm that in many cases intellectual brotherhood is something more than just a simple good desire and that the frontiers and passports many times have nothing to do with our common task: the search for truth.

Commentary

MAGNUS MÖRNER

"The day of 'area specialists' or 'Latin Americanists' is over." The last sentence of Professor Charles Wagley's most stimulating and provocative paper may seem shocking to those of us who have spent considerable time and effort in getting acquainted with research on Latin America outside our own discipline. It may seem shocking, too, considering the large amount of effort and money invested in the training of "area specialists" on different levels. Nevertheless, I believe that Professor Wagley is essentially right in his assessment.

If a "Latin Americanist" does not possess a firm grasp of his own discipline, his smattering of knowledge about other aspects of the regional study is of little scholarly value. The broad perspective should mainly be obtained through one's own discipline. Though it is true that disciplinary boundaries are, indeed, created by the scholars themselves, solid training in *one* discipline is the only kind of insurance there is against amateurism and superficiality. At present, Latin American studies may be in fashion, as Wagley says, but he also predicts that this situation may not last for long. The ultimate achievement of a *stable* position for our regional specialization will largely depend on our capacity to excel within our respective disciplines and to set standards of training and criticism that are sufficiently rigid. Within social anthropology, it is well known that some Latin Americanists played or play a leading role. The situation is different, though, within my own discipline, which is history. Latin Americanist historians have been considerably less conspicuous within their discipline. This, in turn, may have induced fellow historians erroneously to believe that Latin American history is something remote and exotic; in fact, it is just another variety of Western civilization overseas, though, remarkably enough, combining the Western framework with a material backwardness otherwise characteristic of non-Western regions.[1] In the case of Latin American history, at least, our aim must be to get this field fully integrated within our discipline. As long as it is not, the global study "of men in time"[2] will lack in completeness and depth.

Professor Wagley's position on the key issue of area *versus* discipline has many implications. He speaks himself about the almost terrifying growth of the scholarly production on Latin American society in recent years. The need to keep up with what is done within one's own discipline will unavoidably make it still more difficult for one to follow what other disciplines produce on Latin America. Most scholars' time for "input" is very limited. In other words, the need for "cultural brokers" to summarize briefly the state of research on Latin America within one discipline for the benefit of scholars belonging to another discipline becomes greater and greater. It also means that occasional interdisciplinary conferences fulfill a very real need, as is well demonstrated by the present one.[3]

Even so, the researcher will often feel uncertain and frustrated when his topic extends beyond the boundaries of his specific training and knowledge. In his report, Wagley calls for individual research rather than teamwork and group undertakings. But problems of an inter-disciplinary nature will surely meet on the level of very specific projects as well as on the level of projects with a grand design. They may prove very hard to cope with for the individual researcher. Would not teams consisting of two or three researchers representing different disciplines and, hopefully, different nationalities often be the best way out of this dilemma?[4] I fear that it will be difficult to harmonize Professor Wagley's insistence on a high degree of specialization and disciplinary limitation with his stress on individual research. Some research tasks will, no doubt, demand a high degree of professional skill within *more than one* discipline.

Professor Wagley justly points out some of the delicate problems that affect the relation between research on Latin America by outsiders and research by Latin Americans themselves, but he does not suggest a concrete remedy for this dangerous situation. Surely, there is no panacea to be found since these problems are simply integrated parts of the dichotomy of underdevelopment and overdevelopment. But must not this fundamental dichotomy also affect our assessment of research opportunities if we really want our research to be of interest to our Latin American colleagues and to be tested by them?[5] Charles Wagley does not make any explicit mention of this angle of the problem. Also the historians ought to be aware of the present, I think, when they select and approach the problems of the past. But this does not at all mean that the more recent history *per se* would be more relevant to Latin America's present agony than chronologically more distant subjects. A topic related to seventeenth-century land tenure may be infinitely more relevant from this point of view than a nineteenth or even twentieth-century revolution. Therefore, research priorities stated in chronological terms by foundations and academic planners are bound to make little sense, if they are not outright harmful.

I join in Professor Wagley's demand for specialized monographs at this stage since "There are too many theories about Latin America based upon the same monographs and the same old data." If this is true of social anthropology, it is truer still of history, particularly social history. In the United States, many potentially valuable monographs are apparently buried forever in the form of M.A. and Ph.D. dissertations because they would not provide *saleable* books, the curse of an overwhelming commercialization of scholarly publications. It also seems as though an academic teacher would be better-advised to produce a mediocre book on a saleable topic than an excellent article in order to obtain promotion. Even if, theoretically, bibliographies and microfilm would make the dissertations available, I suspect that in practice, more than not, they are only remembered by the author himself and his academic teachers. Such a system seems to me an *inexcusable waste* not only of the author's energy but also of his

informants. Let us also think of his use of research facilities and financial grants. Realistically enough Professor Wagley only lists a number
of research opportunities within his own discipline. Therefore, I shall
only briefly comment on a few areas where the interests of social anthropology and history converge. The principal one is, naturally, ethnohistory, about to form a discipline of its own. But anthropologists using
the data of the ethnohistorians trained within the historical discipline
must be cautioned concerning the controversial nature of some of
their results. The revival of the opposition against the so-called
Berkeley school of historical demography must be noted. Ángel Rosenblat recently presented some very serious criticism of the methods
used by the California scholars which cannot be ignored.[6]

As it would seem just now, the long neglected study of Latin American slavery may in the future even become a victim of overfeeding,
thus reflecting an American rather than a Latin American concern.
Furthermore, historians taking a comparative approach to this topic
at times do not pay attention to the rule, wisely emphasized by Wagley,
that variables be controlled and the subject limited.[7] In his paper, he
mentions the need for plantation community studies. Such studies are
of very great interest to the historians provided that they include a
historical perspective. The same is, naturally, true, for example, of
hacienda community studies. Would not this be an excellent area for
two-man, two-discipline teams?

The historian as well as the political scientist should also note with
great satisfaction the present trend, according to Wagley, towards the
anthropological study of "inter-community networks and other supra
community phenomena." No historian ought to deny the importance
of such links even within the less advanced historical societies. The
study of the role played by religious pilgrimages in Latin America, for
example, opens fascinating perspectives. The other day I happened to
notice that the latest addition to the international community of
Latin Americanist centers is one at the Attila University at Szeged in
Hungary, a center for Latin American *and* Medieval history.[8] Maybe
there *is* something to this somewhat peculiar combination!

It is always dangerously easy to suggest topics that would need
research. There is so much that you would like others to do for you.
Nevertheless, let me just suggest two areas not touched by Wagley,
where the results of historical research would benefit our sisters, or
perhaps half-sisters is a better word, among the social sciences.

First, I refer to the long overdue *critical* analysis of colonial chronicles. So often used by historians and anthropologists alike, these chronicles are often to be found at the bottom of ingenious theories and reconstructions. Most Latin American chronicles are, in fact, still waiting for the painstaking and ruthless criticism that most of their medieval and renaissance European counterparts were submitted to long before 1900.[9] This lag helps to explain why the recent work of Ake Wedin, a young European doctoral candidate, on the Peruvian chronicles, has the significance of a revolution.[10]

The other area that I refer to is the history of technology and science. The expansion of this branch of study within the historical discipline in recent times would deserve to be reflected also within the Latin American specialization. The rather recent work of Eduardo Arcila Farías on the history of engineering in Venezuela is one of the very few major contributions.[11] It seems that other social scientists would also benefit from this kind of historical research.

Let me finally repeat my appreciation of Professor Wagley's most interesting and challenging paper.

NOTES

1. The crucial importance of this combination should be made clear to fellow historians.

2. History as defined by Marc Bloch, *The Historian's Craft* (New York: Vintage Books, 1953), p. 27.

3. Another example was the conference on "Race and Class in Latin America During the National Period" held in New York in December, 1965. Most unfortunately, the Latin American Studies Program of Cornell University has so far been unable to publish the proceedings.

4. A good example of such a two-disciplines, two-nationalities teamwork is Jean Borde and Mario Góngora, *Evolución de la propiedad rural en el Valle del Puangue*, 2 vols. (Santiago, 1956), the work of a French geographer and a Chilean historian.

5. The modern Latin American view is well presented by, for instance, José Honório Rodrigues in Manuel Diégues Júnior and Bryce Wood, eds., *Social Science Research in Latin America* (New York and London: Columbia University Press, 1967), pp. 217–37 and by the same Rodrigues and Gunnar Mendoza in Lewis Hanke, ed., *History of Latin American Civilization. Sources and Interpretations* (Boston, Mass.: Little, Brown and Co., 1967), II, pp. 495–500, pp. 516–23.

6. Ángel Rosenblat, *La población de América en 1492. Viejos y nuevos cálculos* (Mexico City: El Colegio de México, 1967).

7. This weakness can be exemplified by Herbert S. Klein, *Slavery in the Americas. A Comparative Study of Virginia and Cuba* (Chicago, Ill.: University of Chicago Press, 1967). The variable of slave importations, for instance, is simply left out.

8. *Informationsdienst der Arbeitsgemeinschaft Deutsche Lateinamerikaforschung*, no. 4 (Köln-Lindenthal: Universität, Nov. 1967), 20.

9. The heuristical methods received their classical presentation in Ernst Bernheim, *Lehrbuch der historischen Methode und der Geschichte philosophie* (Leipzig, 1889 and later ed.).

10. Ake Wedin, *El concepto de lo incáico y las fuentes. Estudio crítico* (Uppsala, Sweden: Studia Historica Cothoburgensia, 7, Adademiforlaget, 1966). This book and two other studies by Wedin are reviewed in detail in the forthcoming April, 1968 issue of *The Americas* (Academy of American Franciscan History, Washington, D.C.)

11. Eduardo Arcila Farías, *Historia de la ingeniería en Venezuela* (Caracas: Colegio de Ingenieros, 1961).

Commentary

VÍCTOR ALBA It seems to me that without actually saying so, Dr. Wagley raises three basic problems which affect research —and research collaboration—related to Latin America.

Listening to his enumeration of possible themes for anthropological research, each specialist feels the need to add those of his own speciality. I, for example, would point out the urgent need for investigations in oral history (recordings of interviews, etc.) related to the labor movement, to the story of political and social ideas, to the experience in organizing parties, and to the formation of political leaders. The Latin Americans' dislike for filing documents and writing memoirs makes it imperative that we take down the testimony of the survivors of, for example, the beginnings of the labor movement, of populism, or of university reform. Without that, in the future there will be no way to write accurately the social history of Latin America in the past fifty years.

But in this as in the themes suggested by Dr. Wagley and, I am sure, in those that any specialist could suggest, the problems which I have already referred to are immediately raised.

The first is the problem of the orientation of research in the social sciences, economics and history. The confusion which comes from the use of the term "science" in relation to these disciplines leads many— and gives a pretext to others—to believe that they are disciplines which do not have a normative character. Nevertheless, as soon as we begin to write an article or book, as soon as we discuss a published article or book, we immediately discover the normative implications of the research in question. In spite of this we continue to maintain the cliché of "pure science" in our disciplines.

Evidently, it is not a question of suggesting the old (and still so often used) trick of conducting research to support a prejudice or a theory. The orientation which I refer to has to exist, above all, in the selection of subjects. Because the material available is still relatively scarce, we should reject or postpone the subjects which are not in some way related to change. I do not mean that research should be oriented in favor of change or against change, but there should be studies which, in some sense, help us to understand the problems of change.

The second problem, which is related to the first, is that of the function of institutions in aiding research. The most needed studies are, precisely, the most "controversial," those which can give greatest occasion for argument. But in general foundations and universities do not give help to this kind of study. Above all, they do not help studies which can be closely or distantly related to change, not in the sense of something which takes place, but in the sense of something which has to be helped or promoted. We need only point out (without at this time going into the ethical aspects of the matter) that CIA activity in the area of research and cultural activities was owed, above all, to the fact that the need for such activities existed and there was no foundation ready to finance them because they were too controversial. The prime responsibility for the whole CIA mess belongs to the foundations. Researchers have the responsibility of making the foundations understand this and of trying to make them change their criteria.

Finally there is the problem which is raised in the last line of Dr. Wagley's paper: how to use the studies.

I greatly fear that if the day of Latin Americanists is ended, we will condemn the studies which have been carried out to die from boringness in the libraries and files of the specialists. The majority of studies that are being carried out are such, and their specialization is becoming such, that instead of helping one to understand, they cause confusion. To know five hundred fragmentary truths, each one from four to five points of view and disciplines, is not to know the reality in which Latin Americans live. In order to know this the mass of studies has to be synthesized (and I believe, in passing, that a certain amount of coordination among individual studies to make them comparable and congruent would be useful). But synthesis is impossible without synthesizers. In the final account the synthesizers are Latin Americanists. What "area specialists" did in the past with little material (and I don't believe they did it badly), should now be done with this increased amount of material. Perhaps this means that in addition to researchers, each discipline ought to also have its "area specialists" of the field, and that, in the final account, there will appear interdisciplinary "area specialists." Without this, I fear that researchers will end up with a sense of futility and feel frustrated before beginning their work, which will finally become a routine performance for academic requirements or from submission to the slogan "publish or perish."

Not unrelated to all this is the fact that there is almost a complete absence of such synthesizing studies which are basic for giving the researchers the feeling that their work does not lack meaning—by bringing to Latin Americans (and Americans) who are not researchers nor form a part of the academic world the results of this mass of studies.

All studies which are being carried out today in Latin America in our fields are related, in one way or another, to change. With proper synthesis we can make the experience derived from these studies available to technicians, experts, professors, students and leaders. But if we limit ourselves to this, we will only be encouraging one of the possible methods of change: change by action of the élites. It has not been proven that this is the most effective method, nor even preferable, nor that it can give results in Latin America. In any case, it is not for the researchers to make this decision. But by not thinking about how to bring the results of these studies (or better, a synthesis of these studies) to those who are the subjects of change, in reality the researchers decide in favor of change by the action of the élites.

As a result it seems to me that it is urgent to undertake studies of how to bring this mass of knowledge—simplified, of course—to the mass of Latin Americans. However complex it may be, there is no research which cannot be reduced to certain very simple propositions. Understanding them is vital for the leaders, and interesting for the professors and students, but is equally important for those who are studied, for the subjects of change, at any level of Latin American society. But, up to now, there have been no techniques available nor even information about the methods and channels for communicating this kind of information. Without this information we condemn Latin Americans to submission to the élites and researchers to sterility. This double condemnation is too serious to be adopted by simple omission.

An Essay on Interdisciplinary and International Collaboration in Social Science Research in Latin America

KALMAN H. SILVERT

University unrest is a fascinating part of the present world situation of great promise and threat. A certain mystery and romance inhere in Berkeley, the Católica of Chile, Columbia, Warsaw, and the Sorbonne that it would be shameful to cheapen with hasty judgment. There are some apparently common threads, however, not least among them the search for new definitions of academic-civic relations. I should like to explore one small corner of this problem area through an examination of certain implications of a recent move toward collaborative research between North and Latin American scholars. The relation between such research linkages and much more general social problems is not as attenuated as may at first seem the case, especially because any cross-cultural comparisons can suggest to us what kinds of social relationships are "necessary," and which ones are subject to conscious and thus —conceivably—rational choice. That choices can be and must be made in setting new national courses is an awareness impregnating many societies. Perhaps the broad effects of and extreme sensitivity to university commotion is a part of this awareness, a feeling that the disarray of the intellectuals can actually make a social difference. It is for this reason that I dare to stretch what could be a discussion of mechanics and procedures in U.S.-Latin American academic diplomacy to one of the substance of town-gown relations writ large.

I strongly suspect that much of the current faddishness about collaborative research in Latin American social science and about interdisciplinary research and teaching approaches is a respectable political reaction to a real political problem, but that the reaction is little refined and often even less academic. The political reasons for our preoccupation with collaborative research are clear. The Camelot episode precipitated widespread United States reactions, even though long before all was obviously not well in U.S.-Latin American academic diplomacy.[1] Let us not labor the point: we all have heard much about saturation, untrained scholars, ideologically freighted studies, the failure to make research results available to Latin American scholars and concerned agencies, the inapplicability of certain alien techniques and theories to the Latin American "reality," covert intelligence connections, and so forth. Before this wave of recriminations, too, we all were well aware of the great shortage of scholars involved in Latin American studies, that quality was spotty across the disciplines, that some Latin American societies were (and still remain) almost totally unstudied in systematic ways by anyone (whether North or Latin American or European or Asian), and so on. We continue to know that all these statements of the past decade remain true. But there also have been many profound changes. I should like to list some of those changes that appear to me most pertinent for the purposes of this discussion:

First, there has been a physical proliferation and qualitative upgrading of Latin American studies of significant proportions in the United States. The quantitative dimensions can be found perhaps best described in the study documents submitted to the Department of Health, Education, and Welfare in connection with the still unfunded International Education Act, notably that prepared by Bryce Wood. Qualitative aspects are reviewed in *Social Science Research in Latin America*.[2] Greater academic prestige, more scholarships, more students, more articles and books and monographs, and more university-wide

involvement have made Latin American studies an intellectually excit-
ing and rewarding set of fields of study, but have also exacerbated problems of collaboration with Latin Americans.

Second, Latin American social science has been undergoing a revolutionary elaboration in many senses. Empirical sociology was to all in-
tents and purposes born only twenty years ago in Latin America, and
already it has spawned world-famous professionals and appreciable
numbers of competent yeomen as well as camp-followers from market
surveyors to socio-military analysts. Latin American economists have
tried valiantly (if so far probably vainly) to elaborate their own particular economic theories, while anthropologists and archaeologists
have gone up and down in local and international esteem and professional competence for almost half a century now. New waves are ap-
pearing in political science and social psychology, and even the historians are beginning to feel the pinches of their colleagues.[3] As a
result, foreign scholars working in Latin America are finding that areas
of theoretical, ideological, disciplinary, and institutional vested interest
have been staked out where only a few short years ago vast plains
unmarred by enclosures waited to be grazed.

A third important change is in the institutional structure of Latin
American higher education. Through one or another administrative
procedure, major universities in many nations have begun to provide
for research support and to make organizational room for the empirical
social sciences. Semi-private research institutes (sometimes with an
allied training component) have also come into being; the Vargas
Foundation (Brazil), the Di Tella Institute (Argentina), CENDES
(Center for Economic and Social Development Studies, Venezuela),
and El Colegio de México are among the better known examples. This
structural elaboration in higher education, making possible full-time
research staffs, has also been accompanied by a massive enlargement
of student bodies. The combined result is that the recruitment base
for scholars has been effectively broadened at the same time that institutional channels have been opened for at least their partial absorption.[4]

The extent of this institutional growth should not be overstated, of
course, for the culture and the procedures of science are not as yet
firmly established in Latin America—and particularly in the politically
sensitive social sciences. Florestan Fernandes, a distinguished Brazilian
sociologist, has weighed the matter as follows:

> Before converting scientific and technological knowledge into permanent social and cultural influences, the social scientist must mold the inherited existing social institutions or help new ones to emerge, thereby laying the cultural foundations of science and scientific technology, and of education based on both. In some Latin American countries which are more advanced in the urban and industrial revolution, many of the principal conditions already exist for the normal operation and progressive specialization of the social institutions on which the growth of the scientific system depends. Nevertheless, even in these cases there are certain defects which impede the development of scientific research and of its educational and technological applications.[5]

Fourthly, a similar growth—but inside a different institutional set-up —is clearly discernible in the United States. The crisis of the private university and the correlative flowering of state institutions form part of a more generalized student, professorial, and research support explosion reflecting the expansion of knowledge as well as of population. All else being equal, we may expect continuing pressure on the use of Latin America as a research theater.

And, last in this list of major academic changes, we may mention the slow and hesitant growth of Latin American interests in Europe and Asia.[6] As a generalization, it is probably correct to say that European and Asian involvements will grow as a function of their social science sophistication; that is, the more developed the social sciences, the more the tendency to reach for comparative approaches in order to reduce the ethnocentricity of theories derived from the data bases closest to the hands of the social scientists.

These changes, clustered within the post-World War II period, would in themselves have been sufficient to cause stress. However, added to complex political and other large-scale social transformations in the international community as well as within Latin America, their efforts have been profound in many senses far surpassing the relatively mechanistic questions of collaboration and disciplinary organization we are here considering. We cannot analyze the internal changes in Latin America either globally or in such a way as to take into account the many families of occurrences to be observed there. But I hope I will be forgiven some generalizations concerning the political stance of many parts of Latin America and the United States, as well as the role of scholars within that context.

Scholars involved in Latin American affairs have been buffeted by many emotional, intellectual, and ideological currents in the past twenty years. Between 1945 and 1950, as some Latin American countries began expanding their industrial bases within a political context carried on the democratic words of the war, there was general optimism that libertarian processes could be used for the purposes of modernization. As the Cold War settled over the world and conservative military-spawned regimes proliferated in Latin America (roughly to be dated from 1948 in Venezuela and Peru, and spreading thereafter to many other countries), some pessimism set in, broken by seemingly democratic reactions in Argentina, Brazil, Venezuela, and a few other places by the end of the decade. In the academic world partial internationalization of Chilean social science, the rapid emergence of sociology in Argentina, and many similar happenings in other countries gave promise at least of variety and the strength of a dedication to some measure of freedom. The short-lived Kennedy period seemed to fortify these possibilities, at least for North Americans—skeptical as many were. But in the last three or four years a leaden pall seems to have descended on many Latin American intellectuals and their countries. Military dictatorships in Argentina and Brazil, the low and generally unexciting output of the Mexicans (surprisingly backward in the social sciences in any event), the technocratic and applied political attitudes of the Chileans, and many similar situations, add up to an uninspiring picture. In addition, no indigenously Latin American social theories have gained acceptance through the standard procedures of scientific validation. Thus, social science there has remained mimetic; it has not found its own confident self-identification.

I may be accused of personalizing this statement, of allowing my own perceptions to tint, if not taint, the actualities of the matter. Perhaps even though I am attempting to avoid polemics with this warning to myself in mind, I will permit myself to continue these generalizations by attempting to summarize some Latin American views. These attitudes are largely representative of leftist persuasions, for Latin American social science is not yet sufficiently developed to permit many persons of rightist political stance to become empirical social scientists. The most important drift toward conservatism can be noted in the appearance of "apolitical technicians"—in itself an ideological attitude, one that has been popular in Chile and Mexico for at least fifteen years, and is now gaining ground rapidly among the affective refugees of Argentine and Brazilian social science who have remained corporeally at home. But in the main Latin American social scientists are in center to far left ideological camps. These groups are in varying states of disarray. They do not know how to reconcile matters of freedom, civil liberties, and rational political organization with the nature of their oppositions and the processes and procedures of modernization. Their ideologies have been confounded by the subtleties and the crudities of events, and their institutional homes have been invaded physically as well as spiritually.

This state of confusion has been compounded by the United States. Indifference and intervention, pedantic words and development assistance, fellowships to scholars and support to governments that "intervene" in universities, verbal attacks on dictatorship and defense of the principles of non-interventionism and the Dominican Republic and Viet Nam make for a bit of ideological racket. The most developed nation in the hemisphere has become prone to abandon the politics of diplomacy for the directness of military power. The most developed countries of Latin America are under military or other forms of authoritarian rule. Freedom and liberty and democracy are words now used most easily by authoritarians in Latin America, and when heard from the lips of Americans are suspect as either the ingenuities of children or the lies of tyrants' assistants.

It is now time for me to condition these statements. I am well aware that countries like Chile, Uruguay, and Costa Rica exist. I know, too, that no Latin American dictatorship is totalitarian in its sweep. In all countries there are institutional nooks and crannies in which intellectuals may hide, and ways in which free academic inquiry, even on sensitive subjects, can be pursued. In addition, many academic disciplines (law, medicine, agricultural sciences, and so forth) are not practiced by individuals with strong ideological commitment, or else are sufficiently specialized and thus encapsulated that they react but weakly to strong political change. Even in Argentina local social scientists can investigate a wide array of subjects without inviting official sanction; discreet self-censorship permits survival, even if its price is to file off the cutting edge of imaginative innovation. In short, there are variables in the situation: the countries concerned, the nature of the academic community and the particular disciplines that have become advanced, the kind of government, the immediacy and nature of European and United States ties, the scholarly associations and their relations with international entities, and those many other factors describing the relationship between the scholar and the public.

It is against this erratic background that the significance of the moves both toward scholarly collaboration and interdisciplinary research need to be seen. The former can degenerate into a political need rationalized as a scholarly good. The latter is an intellectual and cultural necessity to satisfy the demands of scholarly competence and social relevance. Unless we most carefully and cautiously define what it is we are about, we run a grave risk of squashing the necessary separateness of academic inquiry into the mélange of immediate social need. A rush to put academic freedom and autonomy to the unquestioned service of society as represented by the state is, of course, precisely the way to void the meaning of academic autonomy and freedom, and thus of academic usefulness. If modernization is a process of growing differentiation within growing patterns of social synthesis, then we had best be careful to keep our distinguishing marks and our social responsibilities in balance. Such distinctions are not simple to make when comparing societies of very different levels of institutional development.

The advantages in collaborative research between North and Latin Americans are easy to list: (1) the Latin American may be a distinguished scholar who can test complex theories with sophisticated techniques; (2) the Latin American can supply an institutional base and thus give identity and local sanction to the undertaking; (3) the Latin American can be counted on to supply linguistic help and point out areas of research need; (4) the Latin American component can help assure access to the publics and places to be researched; (5) the Latin American can reduce threats to research continuity; (6) the Latin American can recruit research assistants where needed; (7) the Latin American can point out areas of danger and of security; meanwhile, (8) the North American can supply his usually greater technical and perhaps theoretical competence; (9) the North American can more easily attract research funds; (10) the North American may bring international prestige to the undertaking; (11) the North American may be able to assist in the U.S. training of Latin American students before, during, and after the research period; (12) the North American may extend a measure of political protection to his Latin American colleagues by the symbolism attached to his mere presence in a collaborative arrangement; and (13) the North American may more easily assure publication of the research results.[7] This list does not exhaust the possible benefits. Visiting scholars may offer teaching services, there are gains potentially inherent in merely the facts of interchange, and so on.

Given all these positive elements, why should I counsel caution?

Because, simply put, the mutual advantages tend to hide substantive differences of viewpoint and interest that may well damage the scholarly task in itself. Parsons, in commenting on the political involvements of American scholars, recently pleaded for "a primary commitment to the intellectual task" as the basic dedication no social scientist can afford to forget either in his academic or his citizenship roles. The place of this dedication generally is not the same for North and Latin American scholars. Let us return to the Camelot episode for exemplification. The Chilean academicians who attacked the undertaking were not complaining because Americans work for a government. After all, they themselves recognize no firm distinction between their roles as professors and as aspiring or practicing members of their own state apparatus. Indeed, most of them would argue that it is the absolute duty of the academic to make his services available for the public good, and that the University must be activist in the pursuit of social ends. Their complaint against the Americans is that they were working for the *American* government, and it will not do to excuse their view because the Department of the Army was the particular agency concerned. The criticism is directed as well against the State Department or any other part of the U.S. government involved in sponsoring overseas research.

The reaction in the United States was quite different. Here we raised questions concerning the proper boundary between academic inquiry and government sponsorship.[8] Our reactions concerned university autonomy in its fullest sense; the Latin Americans, despite their historical interest in autonomy, in truth raised but a procedural and political question. The differences boil down to two essential matters: how to create a *relevant* social science; and how to be relevant and retain the integrity of the total academic enterprise. It is my opinion that the Latin Americans are not handling this issue well, and that any ideologically-inspired surrender by North Americans to ingenuous Latin American decisions in this area will lead to a continuing second-rate social science. There are, however, some Latin American scholars who have thought clearly, incisively, and with intellectual elegance on these matters. Notable among them is Florestan Fernandes, whom I have already cited in this connection. He writes:

> Latin American social scientists are obviously striving to intensify scientific research. But so far as the results of such work are concerned, the direct results, which contribute to theoretical advances in the social

sciences, and the indirect ones, which further the progress of the relevant educational and research institutions, it is the indirect results which attract the greatest interest and attention. This means that owing to the conditions under which they work, these scientists must give exceptional weight to results transforming scientific research into a means for achieving other ends. Although these ends are essential for the expansion of science and scientific technology in Latin America, their importance entails choices that may seem strange to the social scientists of the more advanced centers which are mainly or exclusively concerned with theoretical advances.

This fact must be faced with complete frankness if the different positions and evaluations of the foreign Americanist, and of the Latin American social scientists are to be understood. In one way or another, the latter is a conscious agent of social change. His approach to social objectives and activities is that of an innovator in the field of cultural dynamics. . . .[9]

Note, however, that Professor Fernandes is careful to state that the applied aspects of the Latin American social scientists' work should be directed toward the development of the institutions in which his scholarly tasks are to be carried out, and that it is basically in this way that he becomes a responsible agent of social change.

I should like to align myself firmly with those persons who plead for a relevant social science. But let me indicate what I mean by that term—and perhaps my alliance with that group will be rejected by some of its members. It is my view that the integrity of academia *and* its relevance are not separable. The only authority academic commentary on sociopolitical matters can have comes precisely from the methods of study, of expression, and of replication peculiar to the several social disciplines. I trust the personal political views of my colleagues to be objective and "intelligent" no more than I unquestioningly trust the views of my local garbage collector or congressional representative. I do not believe that intellectuals should rush into government service, or that their presence therein guarantees good government. At least one reason is that all too many intellectuals convince themselves that they are possessed of "truth" instead of validity. Indeed, academicians in general and intellectuals in particular are peculiarly equipped to persuade themselves of their own merits. Certainly an inducement to self-delusion comes from the very protections the tenure system builds into academic life. What is supposed to guarantee the freedom of institutional inquiry through the guarantee of individual freedom can be turned to opposite ends by a sanctionless presence outside of the academic world in the political one. Those colleagues who assist governmental policy-making as paid consultants or civil servants, and then defend those policies as members of faculties, are cases in point of a breakdown in institutional differentiation which can only make social science irrelevant under the guise of relevance. To have a policy investment in the consequences of political action is to make it difficult if not impossible to maintain research and teaching objectivity with respect to those policies. A relevant social science then necessarily must be an *academic* one based on a *primary commitment to the intellectual part of the task,* to repeat the phrase.

Latin American social scientists will find it very difficult to be as purist as the above prescription demands. Again to repeat, development implies growing differentiation is partial: class situations, institutional maturation, and social expectations all demand multi-functionality from the more as well as the less educated. Latin American university professors work at many jobs not merely by accident. Societal demands and their own educations permit them to discharge many different functions. Thus, it is natural that they should take advantage of those seams in their societies which bind elevated prestige with academic attainment, political activism, high incomes, and the exercise of the many occupational positions fitting this talent-prestige-income-power construction. Latin American universities are not alone in the dilemma resulting from the universally-jointed professor. Italian students are rioting because, among other complaints, they do not wish academic chairholders to appear once a year and spend the rest of their time in the national legislature, meanwhile drawing their full university pay, small as it may be.

Cross-national collaborative research must of necessity point up differing academic roles, and particularly in the critical matter of the choice of research subject. For example, Latin Americans commonly complain that many North Americans research matters are of no earthly use to them. And many North Americans complain that Latin Americans investigate matters either so abstruse or so applied that comparison and testing are severely hampered. The clash revolves around meaningfulness defined as applicability. And that problem raises the other one—applicability to what, and for what?

Research relevance, social commitment, and professionalism are, to my mind, inevitably linked. I am not of the school that thinks to be "value-free" is to be socially irresponsible in the sense of abandonment of political outlook, activity, and of the politically (or more broadly socially) motivated choice of research subjects. But I would order the matter as follows: all social science inquiry is irrelevant if incompetently accomplished; all social commitment denying the particularity of the scientific enterprise in itself invites the incompetence that guarantees essential irrelevance; all politically motivated research that damages the autonomy and freedom of the professional task is also destructive of competence, and thus assures irrelevance. In short, the irreducible component in the entire game is the maintenance of the scientific commitment *per se*.

It is probably historically valid to say that in the past North American scholars sustained a narrow science-for-its-own-sake approach, while the Latin Americans by and large plumped for a science at the entire service of the public interest as variously defined. This relatively near division has now become blurred. A growing school of American social scientists is trying to reconcile professionalism with social commitment, while a similarly increasing school of Latin Americans is going "technocratic," or "rising above politics," as many social scientists, military officers and others are increasingly putting it in Latin America. The case for the changing North American view has recently been put as follows:

> In effect, thus . . . [I] recommend . . . two things: (1) that in some respects it is not only *logically* necessary to dispense with the Lundbergian idea of differentiating between citizen role and scientific role —it is *wise* to dispense with the idea; and (2) that we view the status "sociologist" as calling for a dual role involving interdependent (a) research-teaching activity, and (b) selected social action activity. Such a view of the sociologist role is simply an assertion that particular types of social action, in addition to other kinds of action, are as proper for the sociologist as is laboratory building for the chemist; neither activity is "pure science," but each is essential to its respective profession.[10]

The author of this quotation adds that public activities supporting the continuing ability of the social sciences to function *as a scientific activity* should be a legitimate area of professional concern. I concur. But what the article does not spell out, and what I consider crucial, is that over any reasonable stretch of time the political mechanisms permitting social science to operate must be libertarian in content. The tug and pull between North and Latin Americans over these points has been subterranean but intense; there is little reason to feel that the

state of disarray in both groups will not contribute to continuing problems. The worry involved is also clear: it is that research collaboration
stemming from political necessity may well lead to permitting Latin
Americans ultimately to judge the subjects to be researched. I find no
prima facie evidence to indicate that those choices will necessarily
fulfill the first condition—the competence condition—for social science
activity. I also find no evidence to indicate that Latin Americans are
particularly competent to define relevance in the more narrow sense,
that they are peculiarly equipped to decide the subjects that public interest imbues with a high priority. For example, more Latin
American governments are (and have been) rightist than leftist.
Where are the studies of rightism? Again, many Latin American economists reject "monetarist" economic theory. Where is the "structuralist"
theory than can compete with "monetarism" on an academic basis?
Where are the political studies needed as an essential ingredient of
structuralist economic thought? To take a third example, more than a
few Latin Americans contend that in the last analysis the United States
controls their destinies. Where is the academic study of the Dominican
episode done by Latin Americans? Of the Guatemalan occurrences of
1954? Of the effects of the Vietnam War on Latin America? Indeed, to
be even cruder, where are the courses taught in Latin American universities on "the United States as area study"?

Significance and relevance used to be handled more simply in the
recent past. Then we told ourselves that economics was the key: indus-
trialize, and then each country could adapt those particular political
institutions and cultural idiosyncrasies it wished within a minimum
level of animal comfort for all. So we deluded ourselves that we could
intervene without interventionism, so to speak. Now that we know that
the very quality of life is somehow involved with economic and all
other kinds of development, we are left with no way of disentangling
development-directed research from judgments concerning the mean-
ings of given institutional patterns and cultural dispositions for social
change. If research is to be relevant to development and modernization, then, it cannot fail to take into some account such intimate matters
as life style and general ways of being. No matter how restricted the
research, if it is to have applicability to problems of change, it will
have implications in extraordinarily delicate areas. The Latin Americans themselves may be avoiding the themes mentioned above precisely because they are so delicate—for them as well as for ourselves.

How, then, are they to be treated? That question is unavoidable if it is relevance we seek. By this time, I hope it will be clear that I do not think the instrumental devices of research collaboration or interdisciplinary approaches will in themselves provide such relevance.

Thus far I have been dialectically counterposing political commitment with professional integrity. Perhaps the search for a "useful social science" (and now let us join the terms consciously) lies in enlarging the areas of meaningful research choices by viewing political commitment and professional integrity not as opposites, but as mutually reinforcing partners. The more that simple professional ends are sought, the less meaningful is the body social to the academic life, and therefore the narrower the range of possible academic endeavor. The more that simple political ends are sought, the less social science is able to provide competent analysis. Social utility and social science utility ultimately demand the same conditions: relativistic, merit-based social systems to support relativistic, merit-based rational undertakings; what is useful to the methods of the latter supports the existence of the former. A truly competent social science investigating truly significant social subjects can in the long run be useful only to rational societies. Social science is thus by this definition irrelevant in the long run to irrational social orders. I will not enter into the argument as to whether an authoritarian society can be a rational one. Empirically, Latin American authoritarianisms have been able to consume "rational" approaches (pragmatically self-testing ones) only in the short run of their first months in office. In intermediate runs they have all fallen over their internal mythmaking. It is small wonder that empirical sociology is invariably the first victim of authoritarian government in Latin America, and that the "technocratic" social "scientists" who lend their services to such regimes quickly end up in jail or consular posts in Belgium. Social science cannot be relevant to anti-scientific governments of the stripe we have seen in Latin America. When we know enough of the social process so that social scientists can be relevant for the establishment of static totalitarianism and thereafter pass into oblivion, we will have arrived at the black utopias of Huxley and Orwell. That kind of relevance is suicide.

In sum, then, my doubts about the efficacy of multidisciplinary and international collaboration stem from my belief that many of the proponents of those approaches are suffering from misplaced hope. They confuse the instrument with the end. No matter the nationalities of the actors or their disciplinary identifications, in the beginning there must be competence and the understanding that professional and social integrity are goals to be simultaneously pursued, for to separate them is to kill both.

NOTES   1. I do not mean to say that Camelot began the move toward such collaboration. The SSRC-ACLS Joint Committee on Latin America, for instance, was discussing and working toward collaborative research at least a year before the Camelot episode.

2. Charles Wagley, ed. (New York: Columbia University Press, 1964).

3. For a qualitative evaluation, see Manuel Diégues Júnior and Bryce Wood, eds., *Social Science Research in Latin America* (New York: Columbia University Press, 1967).

4. There are no reliable statistical surveys at hand to indicate the full magnitude of these changes in size and structure. It would be extremely useful to have for every country such studies as OECD, *Education, Human Resources and Development in Argentina* (Paris: 1961). Incidentally, this survey shows that in Argentina university enrollments jumped from 84,000 to 175,000 between 1950 and 1960 (p. 38).

5. "The Social Sciences in Latin America" in Manuel Diégues Júnior and Bryce Wood, eds., *op. cit.*, p. 22.

6. Many bits and pieces of information about these developments are available in both published and manuscript form. The volumes of the Royal Institute of International Affairs, the reports of the Bellagio conference on European interest in Latin America, Dutch and German periodic inventories, the listings of research given in *Aportes,* and many others are all relevant.

7. This full list of mutual advantages applies most strongly to quantitative studies employing survey research techniques. But elements of this list pertain also to such inherently individual tasks as historical research, anthropological community studies, and so forth.

8. See especially the Fascell and Harris subcommittee reports of both House and Senate, the recent collections edited by Irving Louis Horowitz, *The Life and Death of Project Camelot: Studies in the Relationship Between Social Science and Practical Politics* (Cambridge: Massachusetts Institute of Technology, 1967) and Gideon Sjoberg, *Ethics, Politics, and Social Research* (Cambridge: Schinkman Publishing Company, 1967) and the special issue of the *American Behavioral Scientist,* X, 10 (June 1967) devoted to the proper role of the academic. The matter has been treated consistently in *The American Sociologist,* although no special issue has been given over to the subject.

9. *Op. cit.*, p. 21.

10. Thomas Ford Hoult, ". . . Who Shall Prepare Himself to the Battle," *The American Sociologist,* III, 1 (February 1968): 3.

Commentary

ORLANDO FALS BORDA   It was stimulating and rewarding for me to read Professor Silvert's lucid prose dealing with an important subject on which he is a recognized authority. Collaboration in social science research in its two modalities—interdisciplinary and international —clearly deserves attention from leading figures in the intellectual world of the United States, for well known reasons that do not need to be repeated here.

This seems to be a strategic moment to examine the issues at stake: those dealing with competence, integrity, commitment, and relevancy in the social sciences, as Professor Silvert does. Therefore, we should be grateful for this opportunity. I am also encouraged by his general conclusion that "in the beginning there must be competence and the understanding that professional and social integrity are goals to be simultaneously pursued." I believe that no scholars, even with different cultural, national or political backgrounds, could take issue with these goals. And this is indeed a good sign that collaboration would be possible and that it should become ever more fruitful in all parts of the world, together with its corollaries of information exchange, conferences, symposiums, and cooperative editions on particular subjects.

But this optimism, in order to be realistic, needs to be qualified. The proposed goals are worthy, but they can be pursued in a wide variety of manners. Hence debate is inevitable. Social scientists are far from having a consensus on this tenuous and vital problem. Dr. Silvert has chosen as his support for the first portion of his argument, Talcott Parsons' response to the debate on "value-free sociology" that has been going on during the last few years. The new Parsonian rule holds that a "primary commitment to the intellectual task" should be the basic dedication of the social scientist as a member of academia and as a citizen.[1] Therefore, concludes Professor Silvert, the academic relevancy of social science should be based on that "primary commitment."

Unfortunately, this Parsonian principle appears to have skirted the real issue of commitment, which is at heart a cognitive and existential problem, not merely an academic one. When the problem of commitment is reduced in this manner, it does not help much in illuminating the issues involved in collaborative and other types of research, as I will attempt to show very shortly.[2] Having had to retreat from his previous position on "objectivity," Parsons has now taken refuge in the respectable tradition of the "intellectual task." This rule would be much clearer if anyone had defined the two components of its binomial—intellect and task—and inquired on the nature of the relationships between the two. As the binomial now stands, the scientist's specific task is a mental exercise performed in a vacuum; it is a "purist" abstraction that leads toward the safe and comfortable "ivory tower." The question to be asked is whether the separation of the intellect and task implicit in the Parsonian rule is at all tenable, or rather whether in scientific and academic endeavors intellect and task are inseparably bound together, influencing each other and conditioning methodological preferences, research choices, personal outlook and ideology, and professional competence and integrity.

Of course, this is not the place to resolve this difficult question, and debate on this subject will surely proceed for many more years. However, it may be useful to recall the lead on this question given to us by Max Weber in his monograph on objectivity in the social sciences. The great German master has pointed out how the structural characteristics of his society condition a scientist's explanation of facts; the scientist learns something about the quality of those facts under the orientation provided by his cognitive interest.[3] These elements are inseparable and determine how the process of accumulation of knowledge proceeds. Thus knowledge cannot be viewed as the simple possession of data, but as the creative interaction between the knower and the known, which is another way of saying between the intellectual and his wider task.

Such a flexible approach as well as Weber's own admission of the inevitability of value judgments, which certainly destroys all ivory towers, have been ignored by Weber's own disciples in North America.[4] This is unusual, because such an approach actually belongs in the philosophical and scientific tradition of the United States since the nineteenth century. At least, that, among others, was one of the great contributions of John Dewey in the present one. That this way of looking at the intellectual task is potentially more fruitful for science can be seen from old and current studies which reflect the problems of society and enrich the academic disciplines at the same time. This was precisely the merit of founding fathers of social sciences, like Smith, Comte, Marx, Ward and even Durkheim. This problem is also related to the conception of reality, about which there have been recent developments of some interest. For example, the idea of reality as a "social construct" has been reaffirmed by Berger and Luckmann.[5] A scientist cannot separate his thought-patterns from social reality (especially of the problematic variety), and his explanations would be, in a way, unavoidably shaped by the cultural and social elements that impinge on his personality and training. Moreover, Gellner has recently reminded us that a mechanism that conditions the intellectual conception of reality is language, in the sense that words and concepts that spring from socialization include not only principles to classify things, but also norms, that is, principles to evaluate things.[6]

If these thinkers are right, then the Parsonian rule of the "intellectual task" should be seriously questioned, because it beclouds the central issue of the cognitive and existential nature of the scientific and research problems. Definitely, it needs to be studied further. As it now stands, to attempt to clarify the idea of task in order to separate the intellectual academic endeavor from involvement in the greater society shows a conservative bias that may prove to have frustrating consequences for the advancement of science. Such aloofness of "aseptic science" would reduce the competence of its practitioners, would lead them to choose relatively irrelevant subjects for research, and would cast a doubt on their personal and academic integrity. I will return to these points later on, because they are precisely some of the ingredients in debacles like the Camelot project. Probably, scientists of any nationality formed in this school of thought would be superfluous in a society where they are expected to participate actively (and not only from the academic tower) in achieving a new social order.

Fortunately Professor Silvert, although siding with Parsons, sensed these dangers for his argument and granted that they may have some of the consequences already described. Thus in the second half of his paper he enriches the rule of the intellectual task with the new element of a "social commitment." He writes: "Research relevance, social commitment, and professionalism are, to my mind, inevitably linked." This, I think, would bring him nearer to the position of many social scientists in developing countries who believe that to have a social commitment is not only a most appropriate technique for reconstructing a society, but also a challenging way to build a sound social science. This is a science geared to the needs and goals of society, a discipline which would also fulfill all the scholarly requirements of knowledge accumulation, concept making, and systematization. This challenging position of committed science is supported by contributions of North American scientists like Barrington Moore, Maurice Stein, Louis Wirth, Arthur Vidich, and many others who derived their inspiration from the tradition of dynamic sociology, political sensitivity, and a missionary zeal for change resurrected by C. Wright Mills. These men certainly met Professor Silvert's requirements for competence, relevance, and integrity.

But when Dr. Silvert applies these same criteria to Latin American social science, with the world context in mind, he draws a rather bleak picture, "uninspiring" as he says, showing "states of disarray" and "confusion." He points toward the danger of a "continuing second-rate social science" (south of the Rio Grande) if North Americans "romantically surrender"* to Latin American decisions in selecting research subjects.

I am the first to admit that we, the social scientists of Latin America, still have much to learn in order to become as respected and as skill-

---

* In revising his paper for publication, Dr. Silvert substituted the phrase "ideologically-inspired surrender" for "romantic surrender."—Ed.

ful as, for example, the physical or natural scientists. We started in this race later than most, and our youth still hampers us a bit. This is notwithstanding the fact that the work of many of my Latin colleagues can compare favorably from the technical and many other standpoints with any work by any scholar in any region of the world. In fact, they can competently answer some of the questions posed by Dr. Silvert in regard to economic theory and political studies. Their example as creative, original scholars is worthy of study, because they may be pointing toward a way out of mediocrity seldom seen by most observers, especially by those who, like myself, have followed routinely in the past the North American "aseptic" models of non-committed, aloof science, believing in good faith that such were the highest canons of research methodology. Indeed, it may be interesting to discover that the creativity of some of the best contemporary Latin American scholars appears to go in inverse relation to their dependence on research models and conceptual frameworks devised elsewhere, such as those that have been the routine fashion in North America. In other words, the more creativity and insight for research, the less dependence on the North Americans' current version of the "intellectual task." But this observation should not be surprising because in fact the second-rate social science south of the border may be due to naive imitation of some second-rate theorizing and sterile concept-making devised in, and diffused from, the advanced countries.

Conceptual transplants, unlike grafts of organs in the human body, have not received the attention they deserve. Yet, I believe this issue of acceptance and rejection of new ideas goes to the heart of the problem of collaborative research. Of course, it is inevitable that ideas and concepts diffuse rapidly in sympathetic milieux, and in today's world the fellowship and communication among scientists is closer than ever before. But experience now shows that such readiness of scientific and cultural contacts may have negative as well as positive effects for the intellectual growth of recipient groups. Sheer imitation, apart from the honest desire to confirm a hypothesis, has often proved to be a blind alley, as can be seen in most social science fields in Latin America. For example, in sociology and social psychology the transplant of the equilibrium model to explain local transformations, or of the anomie hypothesis as an automatic dependent variable of urbanization, or of the "n-Ach" measure of attitudes have been, on the whole, unsuccessful; in anthropology, the effort to apply "social indecision" concepts to peasant groups in transition, as well as some bipolar typologies, has proved somewhat barren; in human geography, the Köppen climate classification and the search for "optima loci" have led nowhere; in economics, the theory of the take-off stage of development does not appear to take real hold. On the other hand, I feel that there should be much to learn from the application of principles of social organization to the "forest civilization" and technology being developed by Viet Nam guerrillas; and also from the Cuban social experiments that are proceeding on a big scale, and about which there should be, at least, the natural curiosity of scientists.

Therefore, we scientists on the receiving end now more than ever should exercise caution and good judgment in adapting, imitating, and rejecting foreign models. We should develop a selectivity in concept making with a personal sixth sense for discovering schemes which may not work; or at least develop a *post facto* experimental design to control the diffusion of theories that appear irrelevant or second-rate, thus avoiding further waste of resources and time in their pursuit.

Likewise, we scientists on the receiving end should endeavor to be truly creative and original through the use of autochthonous materials and conceptual leads arising from the specific research situations. Of course, to develop this ability to "fly alone" is an ultimate proof of fruitful scholarship anywhere, and it requires hard work, harder than what we in Latin America have been able to do until now. This task requires that Latin American social scientists "get down to facts," get their hands dirty with local realities, and set a better example of industriousness and productive dedication that would stand up to their colleagues from elsewhere.

For better overall performance, the flow of intellectual interchange should also run the other way, the way least in use today, from the less advanced to the more advanced countries. Scientists in these affluent societies often become involved so much with their own schemes that they may lose the perspective of their immediate realities. Some contemporary developments tend to show that scientists in advanced nations have not been "particularly competent to define relevance in the more narrow sense," that they have not been peculiarly "equipped to decide the subjects that public interest (in the United States or elsewhere) imbues with a high priority." For example, it is hard to understand how United States social scientists were taken by surprise by the local problems of urban unrest, poverty, the rebellion of the young, etc., that have affected or now affect this society. Perhaps contacts with scholars with empathic experience and insight on similar problem areas in developing countries could prove useful in this regard. Independent observers would call the attention of United States scholars to significant problems that have not been tackled in this country, like the role of vested interests and power groups in the continuation of the Viet Nam war, something which is obviously vital for the United States as well as for the world; such contacts would underline the overall lack in North American universities of courses on "the United States as a conflict society," out of which new intellectual stimulation could result.

Thus, the performance of social scientists in developed countries in providing a relevant social science for the present plight of their own societies can be seriously questioned. Sociology, for one, has often been turned into an apology for society and State policies. Then it is only logical to ask oneself, as Dr. Silvert rightly does, what has happened to integrity in science? Has the sense for priorities in scientific research suffered so much in developed countries that newspapermen and amateurs often know more about what is important for today's society than the most sophisticated of its scholars?

Some Latin Americans may be avoiding the themes mentioned by Dr. Silvert because they are so delicate. But fortunately this is not the present trend, and critical studies of society are coming out in increasing numbers. I am unable to see why research collaboration and interdisciplinary approaches could not make a contribution in this regard, especially if partners move within the same frame of reference and abide by the same social commitment. A richer universal science would be the natural outcome of this collaboration. In fact, it is time also that more studies of the United States and other advanced nations in neo-developing stages be made by scientists from late-developing areas. As I have suggested before, the American nation may be needing help and technical assistance from those who have lived or analyzed the problems of underdeveloped societies undergoing subversive processes.[7]

But more than unilateral technical assistance, what is needed is honest partnership. There are many scholars in the United States who not only know about social problems abroad, but also are politically sensitive and empathic about them. Partnership can be productive with such a breed of scholars who have a sympathetic understanding of local ideals. I see in those scholars the beginning of an articulate intellectual counter-elite. And the counter-elite is a healthy sign for the necessary renovation of society.[8] Indeed, this renovation in United States academia is proceeding apace, through new developments like social and political protest movements and the appearance of iconoclastic publications. I admit that I now read more fruitfully journals like *Catalyst* and *The Berkeley Journal of Sociology* than the classic professional ones.

A real sense of partnership in this field of social commitment and serious responsible scholarship is important, but not so essential as an attitude that must always be remembered and stimulated: scientific humility. Intellectual partners in all nations should approach with humble stances the temple of Minerva. This is my plea for this conference: that in order to gain the worthy goals for collaborative research set up by Professor Silvert, we all walk together with a realistic awareness of our difficult task as scientists, for the universe of things we still cannot explain and even less claim to control. And that with our common pursuit for excellence, with mutual respect and assistance we work hard together for a better world through a more efficient and committed *humane* science.

NOTES   1. Talcott Parsons, Editorial, *The American Sociologist,* Vol. 1, No. 4 (1966): 182–84.

2. Orlando Fals Borda, "Ciencia y Compromiso," *Aportes* (Paris), No. 8 (March 1968).

3. Max Weber, *The Methodology of the Social Sciences* (Glencoe: The Free Press, 1949), p. 64.

4. *Ibid.,* p. 10.

5. Peter L. Berger and Thomas Luckmann, *The Social Construction of Reality: A Treatise on the Sociology of Knowledge* (New York: Doubleday and Co., 1966).

6. Ernest Gellner, *Thought and Change* (Chicago: University of Chicago Press, 1964), p. 202.

7. Orlando Fals Borda, "Ideological Biases of North Americans Studying Latin America," New York, December 2, 1966 (mimeo, University Christian Movement).

8. Cf. Orlando Fals Borda, *La subversión en Colombia* (Bogotá: Tercer Mundo and Department of Sociology, 1967); forthcoming English version, *Subversion and Social Change* (New York: Columbia University Press, 1968).

Commentary

STANLEY J. STEIN   Mr. Silvert's essay on the past and present of the social sciences as practiced by Latin American and U.S. scholars is, to say the least, frank and provocative. His conclusion that collaboration should be reduced or avoided because "research collaboration stemming from political necessity may well lead to permitting Latin Americans ultimately to judge the subjects to be researched," grows out of his historical review of the development of the social sciences in Latin America, and, more important, from certain misconceptions or premises. His essay is an exercise in pessimism. However, one man's pessimism may be another's optimism, and an examination of his historical summary and premises may provide an explanation of his pessimism and my optimism.

In his view, social science on Latin America by United States and Latin American scholars has radically changed in the last two decades or slightly more. In the United States, social science has been characterized by growth in output, institutions, financial

resources, faculty, students, and in the quality (or is it rather sophistication?) of publications. In Latin America over the same decades, technical competence has been achieved, although one might question
here why Mr. Silvert refers to Latin America's professionals *and* "yeomen as well as camp-followers" but not to similar groups in the United
States. And with professionalism have come university interest, the
foundation of research institutes, students and growing financial support. Properly he concludes at this point that "we may expect continuing pressure on the use of Latin America as a research theater."

These promising developments are withering, however, in the wind
of the cold war: "a leaden pall seems to have descended on Latin
American intellectuals and their countries." The result is "unexciting"
publications, technocracy and applied political science. It is implicit in
Mr. Silvert's essay that Latin American social scientists have become
nationalists, that they cannot combine professionalism, research relevance and scholarly independence. In a word, integrity and relevance
are subordinated to income and the state, to Mammon and Leviathan.
It is *almost* explicit that United States social scientists have recognized
their fall from grace, that they have compromised their former integrity for national interest, while it *is* explicit that their Latin American
counterparts have always been mired in "the entire service of the
public interest as variously defined," and are only now seeking independence, that is, professionalism and integrity. At this junction, effective collaboration is a chimera, concludes Mr. Silvert, because Latin
American social scientists, masters at last in their house of social
science, cannot combine social relevance, integrity and professionalism.

The argument of Mr. Silvert's essay suffers, it seems to me, from four
major misconceptions or misunderstandings of the past and present
situation of social science research on Latin America.

First, when Mr. Silvert claims that the "irreducible component of
the entire game is the maintenance of the scientific commitment
per se," he is obviously offering an ideal-type of social science. It
is a myth of our nineteenth- and twentieth-century liberalism that
social science research has been, is or will be carried out without
subjection to external forces and without application for national
interests. Among United States social scientists devoted to Latin
America, for example, only a minority have been voices of protests
against the lack of empathy for Latin American problems in the United
States. To be more precise: how many outstanding scholarly studies

by United States scholars do we have of the results of capital flows to Latin America, of the efficacy of the Pan American Union, of the Organization of American States, of the Alliance for Progress, or of the United States interventionist role in Latin America? The minority aside, most United States social scientists, including some of the most professionally or technically competent, have in one sense or another, and now more than ever before, sailed before the winds of state. All I am stating is that the social scientists of the "People of Plenty" have undoubtedly achieved technical competence, but that questions may be raised properly about their relevance, commitment, integrity. More often than not, as an examination of the offprints of Latin American centers flooding our mailboxes shows, the United States output may be categorized as "unexciting," "technocratic" and seemingly if not actually "apolitical." There is more than one glass house at which one may hurl stones.

Second, perhaps it is misinterpreting the present phase of Latin American social science to call it apolitical or technocratic. Perhaps it more properly should be termed a plateau of development, a phase of intense professional recruitment and training, and of the creation and maintenance of institutions and publications. Mr. Silvert mentioned the outstanding ones, El Colegio de México, The Vargas Foundation, the Di Tella Institute, the multifarious Chilean-based centers. We should not overlook the recently founded Latin American Social Science Council, a product of the impressive advance of social science research in Latin America and the need for cooperation among Latin American research centers.

Given the socio-political framework in which Latin American centers must operate, their survival and expansion constitute a substantial and promising advance over earlier conditions. Given their limited resources, and the overpowering presence of social science studies and analytical tools applied to them by foreign scholars, it is entirely understandable why they have as yet not fully developed a "structuralist" theory of economic change, a structuralist-functionalist theory of politics, or a scholarly analysis of United States intervention in Guatemala, or the Dominican Republic. Let us recall that before the United States universities created formal institutional centers for studying Latin America or other foreign areas, they first created centers for the study of American Civilization at Harvard and Yale in the 1930's. Faced with the choice of understanding national or Latin American problems or the United States as area study, Latin American social scientists have logically focused upon their own gardens, particularly in view of the overwhelming hegemony of the United States in their hemisphere.

Third, one should not underestimate the role of the United States in Latin America. There are the visible and invisible pressures of the United States governmental apparatus, as well as those of the United States business community, daily applied to Latin America which constitute something more than what Mr. Silvert calls "a bit of entropy." Can we, in all justice, attack the Chileans for complaining in the Camelot case that Americans were employed by the *American* government, and for neglecting to attack employment by *any* government? If I read correctly the present stance of United States scholars toward involvement with the Institute for Defense Analysis on a number of campuses, they are not abjuring cooperation with the United States government on urban renewal or anti-poverty or anti-pollution campaigns; they are discriminating among varieties of government employment. For Chileans and North Americans, this is hardly insensitivity to the nature and goals of political commitment.

There are, I should also add, the pressures in Latin America stemming from the role of the United States universities, United States research institutes and United States philanthropic foundations which shape the current tendency there toward technical proficiency. To Latin American social scientists there must exist in such intimate collaboration the danger of accepting United States-developed theories, analytical tools and general orientation. Faced by these United States imposed pressures, visible and invisible, governmental and non-governmental, is it any wonder that Latin American research centers strive for independence, for example, by sending their students for training at international organizations in Santiago de Chile or at French and English centers of social science? They seek more, not less, collaboration, but they seek it on their own terms to answer their own problems.

Finally, there seems some confusion in Mr. Silvert's use of the term collaboration. He gives us an excellent and comprehensive catalogue of varieties of United States-Latin American collaboration, from linguistic assistance and delineation of research needs to early publication of research results. He seems to draw the line at collaborative research whose topics or foci must be determined by Latin Americans. While this may be valid, but certainly not beyond dispute, there still exists a broad area of mutual, satisfactory collaboration. For a long time United States social scientists have with only notable and justified exceptions, received sympathetic, disinterested assistance and counsel from Latin American counterparts. Resistance by Latin Americans has been generated by those United States scholars who believe themselves in training as candidates for the status-conferring role of crisis-managers. United States social scientists once warmly collaborated with a foreign scholar Gunnar Myrdal, in the preparation of his masterwork, *An American Dilemma,* because they recognized his professionalism, his integrity, his sense of social relevance. Is it logical (not to say fair) to claim that Latin American scholars would deny today collaboration to a United States scholar engaged in a comparably socially relevant, technically taxing, research design? This is another way of stating that we must consider Latin American and United States social scientists as part of a greater community of seekers after enlightenment. To paraphrase a phrase once employed by Mr. Silvert in *The United States and Latin America* (1959), many roads lead to social science.

Mr. Silvert has pointed to an impasse to effective United States-Latin American collaboration in the social sciences, and he has emphasized those elements in the Latin American scene which lead him to worry about the terms which Latin Americans may dictate as the basis of collaboration. By the same token, he has underplayed the Latin American worry about our terms of collaboration. We should avoid ethnocentrism, the view that somehow we, United States social scientists, have more successfully than others combined professionalism, integrity and social relevance. Ultimately, the interested public will determine how to rank the performance of Latin American and United States social scientists.

Meanwhile, there is reason to be optimistic about the possibilities of collaboration on social science research in Latin America providing we Americans recognize that our intellectual empire in Latin America is receding. Rather than withdrawing into the penumbra of imperial decline in a mood of cynicism, we should join forces with our Latin American colleagues to move toward the light at the end of the tunnel.

Commentary

DIETER K. ZSCHOCK   Kalman Silvert has cogently raised a number of problems whose discussion may lead to controversy and possibly to some new approaches in collaborative research. Collaboration in research among North American and Latin American social scientists is difficult, Silvert argues, and perhaps not even desirable if research objectives do not coincide. Social scientists from North America increasingly choose Latin American settings to apply their theories of pre-industrial societies and of economic development. Their Latin American counterparts, though awed by the scientific approach, nevertheless question the underlying assumptions of theories that are derived from other times and other places. The Latin American social scientist typically has different research priorities, derived from different concerns, and a different approach to asking research questions, than his North American colleague.

The difference, as I see it, is essentially cultural in its substance.

In how they approach research questions, the difference is between the wholistic approach of Latin American scholars and the particularistic approach of North American scholars. The former emphasize the interdependence of problems and needed solutions and question the relevance to the study of Latin American problems of western social science theories. The latter usually prefer to examine segments of the whole and assume *ceteris paribus* conditions. Basically, however, the difference in the study of developmental phenomena involves the ultimate objectives of development. Most educated Latin Americans, at heart, prefer the images of European rather than North American life styles, professing their belief that the attainment of cultural identity is at least as important as materialistic progress.

In addition to cultural differences that predetermine what questions social scientists ask, and how they ask them, Silvert rightly suggests another obstacle to research collaboration. This one concerns the role of the social scientist in his environment, and particularly how he relates to his government. The North American scholar takes for granted his freedom to undertake research and to play the social critic, and he pursues his calling within a supportive environment. He is also expected to advance the methodology of analysis, a skill that makes him sought after by his government which must cope with the complexity of an advanced economy. Not so with his Latin American colleague, who frequently is at odds with his government, who does not have a penchant for scientific approaches to analysis, and whose government relies on foreign experts for technical advice.

There is, of course, an obvious exception to this generalization; I am referring to a numerically small but internationally known and highly regarded group of social scientists from Latin America whose work we consider—perhaps too optimistically—as representative of Latin American social science. Most members of this group hold advanced degrees from North American or European universities. They publish in prestigious foreign journals and attend international conferences. But they have become detached from the daily political confrontations in their home countries. What needs to be recognized, I suggest, is that so far in Latin America the only way to achieve intellectual detachment is to gain international recognition and in effect, to become "internationalized."

In other words, there are really two kinds of Latin American social scientists, namely (a) those with extensive training abroad, and (b) those whose formal education is limited to domestic universities, with perhaps a brief "cram" course at some regional center of training and research, or a "travel and study" grant from a foreign agency. While the former group can afford to become intellectually and geographically detached from its research laboratory, the latter group remains—perforce—completely involved at home and represents, in effect, a part of the environment that is to be studied. It is not difficult to understand—if one recognizes this reality of Latin American political life—why domestically-trained Latin American scholars are mystified by the meaning of scientific research approaches that require personal detachment and independence.

Looking at Latin American politics, there are the "ins" and the "outs" among competing factions of the oligarchy, and then there are those factions that oppose the oligarchy altogether and call for revolutionary change. The former typically differ among each other over what avenue of evolutionary development is preferable, roughly along the structuralist-monetarist dichotomy. The latter differ with each of the former on ideological grounds over the nature of change and the priorities of development. The domestically trained social scientist in Latin America typically is part of one of these factions; he becomes part of the government when his faction is "in," and he is at the mercy of an unstable environment when his faction is "out." Latin America does not, in other words, have a tradition of social scientists who are politically detached. While the ideologically oriented factions are more controversial and therefore more interesting to observe, I disagree with Silvert when he suggests that these factions can claim more or better social scientists than the more traditional factions.

While the U.S. government vacillates over which of many competing political factions to support at any given time, in any one of the Latin American republics, the social scientist from North America is torn in even more ways on the question of collaboration. Should he confine himself to collaboration with the international set of Latin American social scientists? If he also seeks collaboration with the domestic set, should he select his colleagues from among the "in" faction or from one of the "out" factions? In other words, should he follow the lead of his government in the choice of collaborators, or implicitly dissent by collaborating with members of a different faction? Should his research be policy oriented, or should he restrict himself to basic research? Beyond these questions lie others, perhaps more technical, but equally as difficult to resolve. Should he rely on available data and information, or should he develop new primary sources through field work? In seeking collaboration with Latin American counterparts, should he involve them in substantive analysis or restrict them to subservience in mechanical functions? In either case, he must face the probability of dissent on research priorities among his collaborators.

While Silvert advises Latin American social scientists to seek greater intellectual autonomy and to develop their skills in methodology, he also identifies himself with the pursuit of a more relevant social science. Relevance here presumably refers to the selection of research subjects that are generic to the development process. Are we to understand that Silvert recommends that Latin American social scientists should shift their primary commitment from the political to the intellectual part of the development task? Are we to believe, for example, in the possibility that Latin American universities will change their character from being hotbeds of political dissent to becoming towers of academic detachment? In other words, is Latin America developing universities and research centers that can seriously criticize the existing order, and that will do so with the detachment of scientific method rather than through partisan dialectic? And will Latin American governments condone the criticism and seek the technical advice of domestic social scientists, and perhaps gradually phase out the use of foreign advisors? Answers to these questions will vary, depending on one's view of what constitutes progress in the achievement of development objectives.

One can debate this question on various levels. For example, one might ask whether there is, indeed, significant overall progress in attaining developmental objectives and political maturity; in other words, whether the Latin American system tends increasingly toward stability. If this were so, then the role and functions of Latin American social scientists might become more like those of North American social scientists when they work in their own environment. That might be one way in which closer substantive collaboration could evolve. On a lower level of expectation, one might ask if the development of Latin American universities, being advanced along North American lines, holds some promise that "their" social scientists will become more like "ours." As I view developmental prospects in Latin America, my answer is "doubtful" to the first question and "perhaps" to the second question. But then I would ask further, would it be desirable to have Latin American social scientist become more like North American scholars?

Silvert suggests that no Latin American social science has so far emerged that asks relevant questions about Latin American development in a scientific manner. North Americans, on the other hand, while employing scientific technique, have failed so far to ask questions that Latin Americans consider relevant. This, to me, suggests a new approach if we are interested in the furtherance of collaborative research.

Let us bring scientific method to bear on questions that appear relevant to our Latin American colleagues. In the process, we can test the usefulness and applicability of various tools of analysis, as well as the underlying assumptions of our social science theories. Both types of activity would be healthy exercises for North American social scientists to engage in. We can also continue to ask our kinds of questions, but we should engage in a continuing exchange with our Latin American colleagues on what are questions they consider relevant and why. Whether or not we agree on their choice of questions, we should help them to seek answers to those questions.

Latin Americans need to explore whether they are, indeed, asking relevant questions. They need help in seeking answers that are based on scientific analysis rather than on partisan dialect. We, in turn, need to listen to their questions if we ever expect to understand Latin America. We may even find—by testing our methods and theories on questions that others, rather than we ourselves, ask—that our own social science is far from adequate either for the analysis of Latin American problems or even of our own problems. Moreover, an open exchange of opinions on values may do more to enhance prospects for inter-American understanding and collaboration in research than any claim of superiority implicit in unquestioned social science theories, such as North Americans continue to apply in Latin America.

This type of collaboration might help to make research on Latin America more relevant to the region's development tasks; it might also begin to take research itself out of the inter-American political arena. Latin American universities might be able then to develop an indigenous social science. However, I doubt that Latin America is reaching a level of stability at which those of the region's social scientists who are committed to the development task will be inclined to leave politics to others. But North American scholars can help their Latin American colleagues develop scientific skills of analysis, while leaving to them the choice of questions as well as the choice of alternatives among possible conclusions. They may then be helping to produce new leaders capable of accelerating development and of creating an indigenous social science.

NOTES ON CONTRIBUTORS

RICHARD N. ADAMS

Richard Adams is a native of Ann Arbor, Michigan. It was in that city that he undertook his undergraduate education at the University of Michigan. His graduate education was at Yale University, where he received the doctorate in Anthropology in 1951.

After serving as ethnologist with the Smithsonian Institution and anthropologist with the World Health Organization, Dr. Adams taught in the Department of Anthropology and Sociology at Michigan State University for six years prior to joining the Department of Anthropology at the University of Texas. In addition to his appointment as Professor of Anthropology, he served as Assistant Director of the Institute of Latin American Studies at the Austin institution. During the 1960–61 academic year, he was Visiting Professor at the University of California.

Professor Adams has contributed numerous articles to the scholarly journals in his field as well as chapters in edited volumes of essays on social problems and change in Latin America. His own published volumes include: *Un análisis de las creencias y prácticas médicas en un pueblo indígena de Guatemala* (1952); *Cultural Surveys of Panama-Nicaragua-Guatemala-El Salvador-Honduras* (1957); *A Community in the Andes. Problems and Progress in Muquiyauyo* (1959); and *Migraciones internas en Guatemala: expansión agraria de los indígenas Kekchies hacia El Petén* (1965). He co-authored (with Charles Cumberland), *The United States University Co-operation in Latin America* (1960). His edited works include *Political Changes in Guatemalan Indian Communities* (1957); *Social Change in Latin America Today* (1960) and (with D. B. Heath) *Contemporary Cultures and Societies of Latin America: A Reader in the Social Anthropology of Middle and South America and the Caribbean* (1965).

ANTONIO ALATORRE

A native of Autlán, Jalisco, in Mexico, Antonio Alatorre attended preparatory school in Guadalajara prior to undertaking his professional training in the Faculty of Philosophy and Letters of the Universidad Nacional Autónoma de México and El Colegio de México. He presently divides his time as Director of the Centro de Estudios Lingüísticos y Literarios at El Colegio de México and Professor of Spanish at Princeton University.

For the years 1946–48, he studied as a scholarship student in France and Spain. Subsequently, he worked as a translator for the famed editorial house El Fondo de Cultura Económica. Since 1948, he has been a member of the faculty of Philosophy and Letters of the National University. In 1958, he joined the staff of El Colegio de México as an investigator.

Professor Alatorre is the Director and Co-editor of the *Nueva Revista de Filología Hispánica*. In 1956, Agustín Yáñez presented him with the José María Vigil Medal for his achievements as a researcher. His numerous articles have appeared in such distinguished journals as *Cuadernos Americanos, Filosofía y Letras, Revista Mexicana de Literatura, Modern Language Notes* and his own *Nueva Revista de Filología Hispánica*.

His translations have included Ovid's *Heroidas* (1950), Machado de Assis' *Memorias póstumas de Blas Cubas* (1951), and Antonello Gerbi's *La disputa del Nuevo Mundo, historia de una polémica* (1960). His Spanish version of *Erasme et l'Espagne* by Marcel Bataillon made a significant contribution to Hispanic letters. Professor Alatorre has also directed many concerts of Medieval and Golden Age Spanish music.

VÍCTOR ALBA

Born in Barcelona, Spain, Víctor Alba is a citizen of Mexico. He has served as Visiting Professor at the University of Kansas and as Professor at American University in Washington, D.C. and at Kent State University in Ohio. He currently divides his time between the latter institution, where he teaches one semester each year, and Spain.

Sr. Alba has been very active in the efforts to establish a democratic and progressive leadership in Latin America through his association with the democratic leadership training center in Costa Rica and with the Interamerican Regional Organization of Labor (ORIT). However, he is most widely known for the steady stream of publications which has flowed from his pen.

A score of books and *folletos* bear his name. Sr. Alba's major and more recent publications include: *Sleepless Spain* (1949); *Historia del comunismo en América Latina* (1954); *El líder, ensayo sobre el dirigente sindical* (1957); *Esquema histórica del movimiento obrero en América Latina* (1957); *América Latina, un continente ante su porvenir* (1958); *Historia de la Segunda República Española* (1959); *El militarismo: Ensayo sobre un fenómeno políticosocial iberoamericano* (1959); *Las ideas sociales contemporáneas en México* (1960); *Historia del movimiento obrero en América Latina* (1963); *Alliance Without Allies* (1965); *The Mexicans* (1967); and *Politics and the Labor Movement in Latin America* (1968).

CALVIN P. BLAIR

A product of the University of Texas, where he received the doctorate in Economics in 1957, Calvin Blair has been a member of that institution's faculty since 1953. He is at present Professor of Economics and of International Business. He also has served as Visiting Professor at the Graduate School of Business Administration of Harvard University, the Instituto Tecnológico in Monterrey, and the Facultad de Economía of the Universidad de Nuevo León in Mexico. The last-named appointment was as an International Education Exchange Professor in 1959–60.

Professor Blair is well qualified by his own international educational and research experience to deal with the subject at hand. At the University of Texas he has served as the Coordinator of the Latin American Development Program for Ph.D. candidates in Economics and Business Administration and as the faculty advisor for the Texas-Chilean Student Leader Seminar. His professional service includes experience as consultant on economic growth and small industry in Mexico for Arthur D. Little, Inc., on evaluation of Peace Corps programs in Guatemala, and on Foreign Service Officer examinations for the Educational Testing Service.

Dr. Blair's research publications including *Economic Growth Projections for the Dallas, Fort Worth and Houston Trading Areas* (1961), *Big Spring, Texas: A Study of Economic Potential* (co-authored with R. H. Ryan in 1959) and *Fluctuations in United States Imports from Brazil, Colombia, Chile, and Mexico 1919–1954* (1959). He contributed a chapter entitled "Nacional Financiera: Entrepreneurship in a Mixed Economy" to *Public Policy and Private Enterprise* edited in 1964 by Raymond Vernon.

HOWARD F. CLINE

Howard Cline was born in Detroit and educated in Harvard. Since 1952, he has served as Director of the Hispanic Foundation of the Library of Congress which, under his direction, has stimulated and assisted individual scholars, institutional programs and professional organizations.

During his graduate days at Harvard, Dr. Cline was a Frederick Sheldon Prize Fellow and recipient of a Social Science Research Council pre-doctoral fellowship. Graduated with honors, receiving the doctorate in 1943, he was for four years, 1944–47, Assistant Dean of the College at Harvard. He taught as a member of the faculties of Yale and Northwestern University before assuming his present position.

Dr. Cline has served as United States representative or delegation adviser at numerous international meetings. He was until recently the United States national member of the Commission on History of the Pan American Institute of Geography and History. His other professional activities include the elected Chairmanship of the Conference on Latin American History and Chairmanship of the Committee on Scholarly Resources of the Latin American Studies Association. He has been a member of the Board of Editors of the *Hispanic American Historical Review* and of the editorial board of the *Middle American Indians Handbook*.

Author of more than fifty major articles and books, Cline's major scholarly publications include the following volumes: *The United States and Mexico* (1953), *Mexico. Revolution to Evolution, 1940–60* (1962), and *Latin American History: Essays on Its Study and Teaching, 1898–1965*, 2 vols. (ed. in 1967).

FRANK DAUSTER

Born in Irvington, New Jersey, Frank Dauster received the B.A. degree from Rutgers University, where he also completed his initial graduate degree. He received his doctorate from Yale University in 1953. He has taught at Wesleyan University and is presently Professor of Romance Languages at Rutgers.

Professor Dauster serves as Associate Editor of *Hispania* and as a member of the Editorial Board of the *Revista Iberoamericana;* he is the Contributing Editor in Modern Drama for the *Handbook of Latin American Studies.*

Scholarly articles by Professor Dauster have appeared in *Hispania, Revista Iberoamericana, La Palabras y el Hombre*, and *Asomante*, to mention only a few. His published volumes includes: *Breve historia de la poesía mexicana* (1956), *Ensayos sobre la poesía mexicana* (1963), *Historia del teatro hispanoamericano; siglos XIX–XX* (1966) and *Tres piezas* (text ed., 1965).

Professor Dauster has been the recipient of a grant from the Social Science Research Council and of the Cady Prize from Yale University.

ORLANDO FALS BORDA

Professor Orlando Fals Borda was born in Barranquilla, Colombia. He was educated at three North American universities—Dubuque, Minnesota, and Florida, receiving his doctorate from the last named in 1955. He has a notable record as a scholar, educator, and international administrator.

His public and international service includes assignments as Assistant Chief of Studies of the International Cooperation Administration in Bogotá, United Nations advisor on rural problems and housing in Brazil, Director-General of the Colombian Ministry of Agriculture, and President of the Technical Council of the Agrarian Reform Institute of Colombia. He also has served as consultant to the Land Tenure Center at the University of Wisconsin, the World Council of Churches at Geneva, and the Social Science Research Council.

Professor Fals Borda is a member of the Executive Committee of the Latin American Social Science Council. He founded and served as the first dean of the Faculty of Sociology of the National University of Colombia. In addition to his appointment as Professor of Sociology at the Bogotá institution, he also has been a Visiting Professor at the University of Wisconsin, Columbia University and the University of London.

Recognitions accorded Dr. Fals Borda include two Guggenheim Fellowships and selection as President of the Colombian Sociological Association and Vice President of the Latin American Sociological Association. He is the author of numerous articles, reports, and chapters in volumes edited by others. Three significant volumes by professor Fals Borda are: *Peasant Society in the Colombian Andes, A Sociological Study of Saucío* (2nd. ed., 1962); *La violencia en Colombia, estudio de un proceso social,* 2 vols. (1962, 1964); and *La subversión en Colombia: Visión del cambio social en la historia* (1967).

MAGNUS MÖRNER

Professor Magnus Mörner was born and educated in Sweden, receiving his doctorate at the University of Stockholm in 1954. From 1953 until 1965, he served as Director of the Library and Institute of Latin American Studies at Stockholm.

During part of his tenure as Director of the Latin American Collection and Program, Dr. Mörner also served as a Lecturer on the faculty of the University of Stockholm. Between 1963 and 1966, he was successively Visiting Professor at the University of California in Los Angeles, Cornell University, and Columbia University. In the fall of 1966, he assumed the post of Professor of History at Queens College and the City University of New York. In 1969 he returned to the Institute at Stockholm.

Professor Mörner was awarded a research fellowship from the Rockefeller Foundation and the award of the Loubat Prize, both in 1958. He holds corresponding memberships in the Academia Nacional de la Historia (Buenos

Aires), Instituto Histórico y Geográfico (Montevideo), and the Hispanic Society of America (New York).

In addition to more than three score articles and reviews, Dr. Mörner has published the following volumes: *The Political and Economic Activities of the Jesuits in the La Plata Region* (1953); *Lateinamerika, Natur & Kultur* (1957); *Leve revolutionen. Tradition och dynamik i latinamerikanskt samhallsliv. Natur & Kultur* (1960); and *Race Mixture in the History of Latin America* (1967). In addition, he has edited *Carl August Gosselman: Informes sobre los estados sudamericanos en los años de 1837 y 1838* (1962) and *The Expulsion of the Jesuits from Latin America* (1965).

RICHARD M. MORSE

Professor of History and Chairman of the Council of Latin American Studies at Yale University, Richard Morse received his bachelor's degree from Princeton and did his graduate work at Columbia University where he received the doctorate in 1952.

From 1949–58 he taught at Columbia University. Subsequently he served as Director of the Institute of Caribbean Studies at the University of Puerto Rico and as Professor of History and Chairman of the Department at the State University of New York on Long Island (subsequently designated "at Stony Brook") prior to going to New Haven. He has been a Visiting Professor at Harvard, Brooklyn College and Columbia.

His professional service includes assignment as Consultant on Latin America to the Ford Foundation from 1958 through 1964, membership on the Board of Editors of the *Hispanic American Historical Review,* and advisory editorship of *Caribbean Studies.* In 1968 he served as elected Vice-Chairman of the Conference on Latin American History, assuming the post of Chairman in 1969. He has been the recipient of grants from the United States Department of State and the Social Science Research Council as well as a Guggenheim Fellowship.

Professor Morse served as editorial chairman for the publication of the *Introduction to Contemporary Civilization in the West,* 2 vols., and *Chapters in Western Civilization,* 2 vols., (1954) and as co-editor of *Man in Contemporary Society,* 2 vols., (1955). He also co-authored with Louis Hartz, et al., *The Founding of New Societies* (1964). His most important work to date is entitled *From Community to Metropolis: A Biography of São Paulo* (1958). Recently he edited with an introduction *The Bandeirantes: The Historical Role of the Brazilian Pathfinders* (1965).

KALMAN H. SILVERT

Born in Bryn Mawr, Pennsylvania, Kalman Silvert completed both his undergraduate and graduate studies at the University of Pennsylvania, receiving his doctorate in 1948. During his academic career he has served as Professor of Government at Tulane University, Dartmouth College and New York University.

For a dozen years during which he served as a faculty member at Tulane and Dartmouth, Dr. Silvert also was Staff Associate to the Director of Studies of the American Universities Field Staff. In 1967 he joined the faculty of New York University as Professor of Government and Director of the Ibero-American Center. Simultaneously he assumed the post of Program Advisor in the Social Sciences and Humanities for Latin America at the Ford Foundation.

Dr. Silvert was elected the first president of the Latin American Studies Association. His publications, which have contributed significantly to the social sciences literature on Latin America, include more than a score of articles in journals and some forty reports for the American Field Service Staff. He is the author of eight chapters in published volumes edited by other authors and three monographs.

He himself has written four books and edited and contributed to three others. The published volumes are: *A Study in Government: Guatemala* (1958); *The Conflict Society: Reaction and Revolution in Latin America* (1961); *Chile Yesterday and Today* (1965); and *La política del desarrollo* (1966). The volumes edited by Professor Silvert are entitled: *Expectant Peoples: Nationalism and Development* (1967); *Discussion at Bellagio: The Political Alternatives of Development* (1964); and *Churches and States: The Religious Institution and Modernization* (1967).

STANLEY J. STEIN

Stanley Stein was born in New York and educated at the City College and Harvard University. He received the Ph.D. degree from the latter institution in 1951. Two years later he joined the faculty of Princeton where he continues to serve as Professor of History.

Recipient of a Social Science Research Council fellowship for research in Brazil, Professor Stein also has been a Woodbury Lowery Fellow and a Research Fellow of the Research Center in Entrepreneurial History at Harvard (1950–53). He has been a member of the Joint Committee on Latin

American Studies of the Social Science Research Council and the American Council of Learned Societies and of the Translation Committee of the Association of American University Presses.

In addition to several outstanding articles in scholarly journals including the Brazilian essay in the histographical series published in *The Hispanic American Historical Review,* Dr. Stein is the author of two books: *Vassouras, a Brazilian Coffee County, 1850–1900* and *The Brazilian Cotton Manufacture: Textile Enterprise in an Underdeveloped Area,* both published in 1957.

CHARLES WAGLEY

Since 1961 Director of the Institute of Latin American Studies at Columbia University, Professor Charles Wagley was born in Clarksville, Texas. He undertook both his undergraduate and graduate studies at Columbia, receiving the Ph.D. in Anthropology in 1941.

The year before receiving his doctorate he began his long service as a member of the faculty of Columbia. His professional experience includes serving as a research associate with the National Museum of Brazil (1941–42), director of the field staff of the Institute of Inter-American Affairs in Brazil from 1942–45, and membership on the staff of the Guggenheim Foundation (1945 to 1947), and of the Social Science Research Council (1947–49).

He has received an honorary degree from the University of Bahia, the award of the Order of the Southern Cross by the Brazilian Government, and has been designated as a Fulbright Scholar to Brazil and as a fellow of the Center for Advanced Study in the Behavioral Sciences. He is a fellow of the American Anthropological Association and of the Ethnological Society, serving as president of the latter organization in 1957–58.

Professor Wagley is the author of the following studies: *Economics of a Guatemalan Village* (1941), *Amazon Town: A Study of Man in the Tropics* (1953, 1964), and *Introduction to Brazil* (1963). In 1964 he edited an important volume of essays on *Social Science Research on Latin America.*

LEOPOLDO ZEA AGUILAR

Leopoldo Zea, philosopher and educator, was born in the Mexican capital. He has served as a professor of the Escuela Nacional Preparatoria, the Escuela Normal de Maestros and, since 1944, the Faculty of Philosophy and

Letters of the Universidad Nacional Autónoma de México. He currently is serving as the Director of this pivotal faculty of the National University as well as Director of the newly established Centro de Estudios Latinoamericanos.

He served also as head of the Department of University Studies of the Secretariat of Public Education in 1953–54 and subsequently as Director-General of Cultural Relations in the Secretariat of Foreign Relations. In 1940 he served as Editor of the review *Tierra Nueva*. Since 1963 he has been the Director of the journal *Revista Philosophia*. Two years earlier he assumed the post of Vice President of the Commission on History of the Pan American Institute of Geography and History.

Professor Zea has published almost a score of volumes on philosophy, history, and the history of ideas. His principal writings include: *El positivismo en México* (1943), *Apogeo y decadencia del positivismo en México* (1944), *Ensayos sobre filosofía en la historia* (1948), *Conciencia y posibilidad del mexicano* (1952), *La filosofía en México* (1955), *Del liberalismo a la revolución en la educación mexicana* (1956), *El pensamiento en latinoamérica* (1963) and *Antología de la filosofía latinoamericana contemporánea* (1968).

DIETER K. ZSCHOCK

Dieter Zschock studied at Wesleyan University before initiating his graduate career at the Fletcher School of Law and Diplomacy. He received his doctorate from the Fletcher School in 1967 with a dissertation entitled "Employment Expansion and Manpower Requirements in Colombia."

Since 1966 he has been a member of the faculty of the Department of Economics of the State University of New York at Stony Brook, and also has served as Acting Director of the Economic Research Bureau and Assistant to the Executive Vice President of Stony Brook. He has been a consultant for the Milbank Memorial Fund, the Woodrow Wilson School of Princeton University, the Agency for International Development and the Ford Foundation.

Prior to joining the faculty at Stony Brook, Dr. Zschock was successively a Training Associate with the Latin American Program of the Ford Foundation on overseas assignment in Colombia and a Research Associate of the Industrial Relations Section at Princeton University. His published research includes *Manpower Perspective of Colombia* (1967) and *Brookhaven in Transition: Studies of Town Planning Issues* (1968) to which Dr. Zschock contributed a study in addition to editing the booklet.

Professor Zschock's forthcoming essay "Economic Aspects of Health Needs in Colombia," will be included in the Proceedings of the "Round Table on Social Science and Health Planning: Culture, Disease, and Health Services in Colombia" (held in New York in October 1967), and in the volume which he is editing under the title *Economic Aspects of Suburban Growth.*